THE GENTLE TOUCH

CHARLES J. KEATING

The Gentle Touch

TWENTY-THIRD PUBLICATIONS
Mystic, Connecticut

Twenty-Third Publications
P.O. Box 180
Mystic CT 06355
(203) 536-2611

Library of Congress Catalog Card Number 84-51585
ISBN 0-89622-217-9

Cover photo by John Simonelli
Cover design by Bill Baker
Edited and designed by John G. van Bemmel

To
Christopher Charles
my son of the Gentle Touch
of seven months

CONTENTS

INTRODUCTION

*P*rovocation is a nasty word. It means that we make others behave in ways they do not want to behave. No one wants a *provocateur* for a neighbor. I would be less than honest if I did not admit that I am trying to be a *provocateur*. This book is written to provoke reflection. I want us to look at life's common experiences and to think about their significance. I'm not sure I have the wisdom to lead. I am more certain I can ask the questions that all of us need to answer at one time or another.

Who am I? Is life worth living? Why? What makes life significant? Where is joy? What does death mean? How do I make sense out of failure? What do I mean when I say I believe? Do I need to believe? Is there life beyond "family"? If so, what does it look like? Why is it important to relate to others? What does the future hold for me?

Believer or not, religious or not, these are questions that come to all of us, questions unbidden and unprovoked. We can smother them, and we are the losers. We can say we do not have the education to deal with them, and we run away. But they are persistent, as persistent as the faith of the believer. Believer or not, we want to make sense out of life. There is more to life than the mortgage, the kids, and insurance. There's retirement. But what do we make out of that? If our life has been a blocking out of meaning, how do we expect to find significance in sleeping late and doing nothing?

I do not want to lead. I do not want to give answers. I want to share a few reflections with you, reflections I need to share because of my own needs.

For over a decade I prepared for a career of service to others. For twenty years I served. I never regret that preparation and service. It was successful and beneficial to myself and to others. But

9

I do not think that we can serve others for that amount of time without questions. There is too much time to think. Not every minister would agree with me. Some of my profession value thinking only in its absence. Activity is the "name of the game." I don't agree.

My experience has been, and continues to be, with God. God is difficult to hear in the midst of activity. Activity tends to be noisy. I have found God in the gentle touch.

> He Who is the mighty Bear,
> Who seldom ventures from His lair,
> Is also the gentle butterfly,
> Who flits about in His "random" way,
> Stroking gently whomever He may.
>
> Perhaps He's flogged you with tong and leather;
> With me, He seemed to always use a feather!

Perhaps I have talked to myself too long, perceiving my self-indulgence to be his Word. That's possible. Maybe you have done the same.

I believe that God still talks to each of us. I believe in ongoing revelation. The gospels will not be finalized until the last person has entered into God's presence. All that has been revealed, all that has been preached, has to be cauterized by our own experience. Like Paul, we are expected to allow the burning of dross that is only dead weight. But I have not felt the burn of the fire. I have experienced the touch of the feather. Perhaps I have been lucky to feel it.

Jesus speaks to us through our children, our wives, our husbands, our friends, our jobs, our interests, and our dreams. Otherwise, the resurrection is meaningless. Otherwise, he is no different from any historical leader whose ideas, like wine, become sour with time. Jesus is ever the new wine at optimum body and bouquet. Because he lives. This book is another effort to make the feather of Jesus felt. I am sure he lives in institutions, in churches, and in families. I am equally sure he lives in the common experiences of all of our lives.

I speak of him in terms of meetings, in terms of connections that are the common experiences of all of us. All of us have felt we have met God at one time or another. If it was not God, then it was a strange, unexplainable experience that we chose to forget or to interpret for change or for oblivion. I want to awaken that experience. We met God in failure, in uncertainty, in another, in love, in joy, in loneliness, in pressures, in dreams, and in our sexuality. But we may not have identified him. I want to share with you how I have sensed him in my own life, with the hope that others will identify with me and enjoy the touch of the feather.

But you do not believe in God. I write for you, too, because I know that you are curious. Who is the spirit of Jesus? Why does belief seem to make a difference? Could it make a difference in my life? To ask such questions is only human. There must be more. I write to share with you what I believe is more.

I offer outlines and a précis that you must complete. My thoughts are random and disparate, leaving room for you to color and to give body. I intend to be provocative, to make you think, to disagree, and to discount. But I want to share what is most important to me.

MEETING
GOD

I have studied *about* God for forty-seven years. I have *met* God for a few minutes on two occasions. The first was in the midst of a worship convention during a celebration of prayer. Since I was responsible for the convention, burdened with all of the details you can imagine, God was the last person I expected to meet. My experience was not emotional or traumatic. The meeting is as real to me today as it was over twenty years ago. He was present. That's it! Nothing more. In the midst of the service, Jesus became a reality to me. There was no need to do or say anything. In the presence of Jesus, it is only important to be. So I was. And I shall never be the same again. Without presumption, I believe that apostasy is unlikely for me.

In his presence, nothing was important. There was tranquillity, peace, and rest. Righteous anger, outraged justice, rights, and demands had no significance. It was only important to be. He was pleased with that. And I was at rest. There is no way I can prove this experience, nor do I want to. I only want to share it. Some have called it a baptism of the spirit, but I do not even want to label it. I am simply grateful for it.

The second time I met God was in an architect, an alcoholic who had found sobriety. While I have never forgotten him, I have forgotten many of the details of our meeting. We were both scheduled for lectures at the same conference. We met in a cocktail lounge in the conference hotel, he sipping ginger ale while I had a Scotch. He spoke openly of his life, his struggle with drink and his current work, expanding a Cistercian monastery in France.

He was gentle. He was open and vulnerable. He was accepting. He did not judge. And he heard what others said. I'm sure I met others with these qualities, but I remember seeing Christ in this man. I said good-bye to him with reluctance. Perhaps I cannot articulate what made him Christ-like to me because God is indescribable, unutterable: he is who he is. The moment of meeting is as real to me now as it was then. For me, it is incarnation.

I now find God in my son, a three-year-old whom I have cared for from nine to five since he was five months old. He gives love without demand. He kissed my wrist as I changed his diapers. He hugs me as I dress him. He loves me for being.

I imagine him having had a conference with God before he came to us. God said, "Show them how much I love them!" "How?" said Patrick. "Give them affection, kisses, hugs when they least expect it. Be warm in their arms and demanding for their attention. Show them you need them." "O.K." said Patrick. And that is what he has done. He has been, and continues to be, a great incarnation of God's love for us. He is "sent," an apostle.

God has never been to me a hurler of thunderbolts, a wielder of swords, or a cause of disease. I always felt uneasy with the plagues of Egypt, while at the same time I have accepted the possibility that God needs to deal with some people in that fashion. So far, he has dealt gently with me and mine.

My favorite picture of God, discovered over a four year study of Scripture, is that of Elijah as he fled the wrath of Jezebel, the wife of Ahab. Elijah had "put to the sword" the prophets of Jezebel. She promises that he will suffer the same fate. He flees, fed and encouraged by the angel of the Lord in the desert. He arrives at the "mountain of God," Horeb, and takes refuge in a cave.

> Then the word of Yahweh came to him saying, "What are you doing here, Elijah?"...Then he was told, "Go out and stand on the mountain before Yahweh." Then Yahweh himself went by. There came a mighty wind, so strong it tore the mountains and shattered the rocks before Yahweh. But Yahweh was not in the wind. After the wind came an earthquake. After the earth-

quake came a fire. But Yahweh was not in the fire. And
after the fire there came the sound of a gentle breeze.
And when Elijah heard this, he covered his face with
his cloak and went out and stood at the entrance of
the cave. Then a voice came to him which said "What
are you doing here, Elijah?" (I Kings 19:9–13)

Elijah discovered God in the gentle touch. In the *Jerusalem
Bible,* the Scripture commentators warn us that this means only
that God is a spirit and that he communicates intimately with his
prophets. It "does not mean that God's dealings are gentle or
unperceived" (p. 447). They point out that God's gentleness is
refuted by the commission to anoint kings who will kill by the
sword the enemies of Elijah and Yahweh. Such a commission
follows immediately on the incident quoted above.

I do not question the scholarship of the commentators. My
experience questions them. I do not think I am a prophet; only,
perhaps, a would-be prophet. But my experience of God, outside of the two events of God's presence in a prayer celebration
and in an architect, has been an experience of the "gentle breeze."

He has revealed himself to me in the midst of workshops,
where I found my hidden drives and inner talents, in friends who
questioned my motives and in enemies who labeled them, in family that silently supported my actions they did not understand,
and in oceans, landscapes, and gardens that cleared my thinking. These have been the "gentle breezes" in which God has
spoken to me, and I to him.

From half a century of observation, it seems to me that God
meets most of us in the "gentle breeze," a gentle touch to which
we may often be insensitive. The cynic might say, and I might
say occasionally, that we are talking to ourselves when we find
God is so agreeable to our thinking. Much prayer is, perhaps,
self talking to self. But we think it is God speaking to us. The
Charismatics emphasize the importance of "discerning the Spirit,"
distinguishing God's voice from our own. I think they have a
point. It is a gift that is sorely needed by many of us believers.
The most dangerous person in the world at any given time is the
person who is convinced that God's voice is his own.

Contrary to the Scripture commentators mentioned above,

it seems that God's voice often goes unperceived. He does speak
gently. He is easy to "drown out." We humans can speak more
loudly and with greater persuasion. We seek to convince. God
invites.

It is possible to find God in institutions, be they "in God,"
"under God," or the "body of Christ." The saints attest to this
possibility. For many, however, such a possibility is weak and
unpromising. At the same time, these same "many" are insensitive to the gentle touch of God in their lives. The marriage
celebration ends with the honeymoon. We do not see God's gift
of himself to each of us in our gift of self to each other. Intellec-
tually, we accept the need of God to support his creation second
by second. We know he is like the movie projector that always
needs to be operating if the picture is to remain. But we think
that our gift of ourself to another is full and finished after a week
or two of marriage. We ignore the gentle touch that suggests marriage needs to be given anew second by second. His message is
unperceived. God has told us that his ways are not our ways,
but he also made us "to his image and likeness." Many of his
gentle touches ask us to be more like him. That is wisdom, the
message of the incarnation. It is not arrogant.

The problem with an institutional God is that he directs us
to the institution. It is natural that the institution strive for its own
survival. In a sense, institutions are legitimately self-serving.
Especially when they seek to serve the needs of people. An institution should not be made little of; institutions are very difficult to establish and even more difficult to maintain. Still, survival is often paramount in the institution's mind. This may be
particularly true of the Christian Church, since Jesus guaranteed,
"I am with you always; yes, to the end of time." (Matthew 18:20b)
And he promised that "the gates of the underworld can never
hold out against it." (Matthew 16:18b) Against this background
it is easy to understand why church members may sometimes
forget to be loving and compassionate when the institution is
threatened. Hence, the seemingly harsh treatment of heretics and
schismatics in Christian history. What aided the survival of the
instutition was the work of God.

Still, God is found in the institution. Much holiness resides
in the homes of church-goers, in parsonages, rectories, and con-

vents today. Holiness is also found among those for whom family and friends are the core of their relationship with God. Some
of us call him God. Some of us aren't sure what to call him. But
we feel his presence in our lives: in births, love-making, family
routine, close friendships, new discoveries, celebrations of joy
and celebrations of sorrow, in deaths, in loneliness, and in our
dreams. He is the gentle breeze that whispers through our lives.
God, in whatever form, gives meaning to the lives of us who try
to perceive him.

Maslow, in his research of "peak experiences," events in
which people experienced the mystical universality of all creation, found that unbelievers had such mystical experiences more
frequently than believers. I do not recall him offering any explanation for his findings. I would venture that believers might have
it too easy. We find God in his Church, in the Bible; we find him
in an institution. So we stop looking. We don't seek him out in
life events, in friendships, or in chance meetings. His gentle touch
goes unnoticed. We have him elsewhere. We do not perceive the
search as the discovery. For those who have found, there is no
need to search.

At the age of eighteen, Thomas Aquinas wrote a short essay
on the philosophical notion of essence and existence. It is of interest only to philosophers, except for his beginning, which is
universal. He wrote, "A small mistake in the beginning is a great
one in the end. . . ." He was paraphrasing another great
philosopher, Aristotle. In spite of the adolescent wisdom of
Aquinas, he is said on his deathbed to have valued his work only
as "straw."*

Thomas speaks for most of us. In spite of all of our efforts
to make sense out of life, to find meaning in what we become
involved in and to find fulfillment, most of us have made a small
mistake in the beginning. We find it later, or we pretend it never
happened. We "stick it out."

Perhaps it need not be so. God is present. He needs us and
he doesn't need us. We are arrogant to think that what we do
makes a difference. We are mistaken if we evaluate our efforts
as insignificant. All of us work "in the dark." Thomas Aquinas

*On Being and Essence (Toronto, Canada: The Pontifical Institute of Medieval Studies, 1949), 25.

17

made a significant contribution to human thinking in spite of his deathbed evaluation. His Judaeo-Christian philosophy led humankind to hospital care, welfare programs, respect for life, awareness of mortality, and the value of human civilization for all groups of people.

God is present where there is love. Essentially Aquinas spoke love. He is obscured by his institutional, philosophical method. Many believers find ourselves in the same confines, although less sophisticated.

We tend to "use" one another. We want others to fill our needs, to support our potential and to meet our demands. We pretend to do that for them.

Our mistake, about which Aquinas warned us, is in the beginning. We are not for others to serve. We are for others. My guess is that Jerry Lewis and Danny Thomas would admit so much: they have found fulfillment in giving to others. Nothing is less attractive initially. Nothing is more fulfilling finally. Meeting God is ecstasy, Greek for "getting out of ourselves." It may be that we then find God and infinity.

I do not know this. I suggest it. We find God in unity, physical or mystical, sexual or spiritual. Of one thing I am sure: we need to be sensitive to the happening.

> Is ecstasy infinity?
> Bodies joined in world harmony,
> A harmony of creation, of beauty, of strength,
> Breaking out, farther, farther, farther,
>> Straining to fly beyond the
>> Flesh to eternal Spirit.

> Is that infinity,
> The infinity of boundless life and growth,
> The infinity that knows no limit or mortality,
> The infinity of God?

> For you, it may be so.
> For another, it may not be.
> Still, for both of us
> It tastes like infinity.

18

Is ecstasy infinity?

To taste is not to appreciate, to grasp, to accept. Millions of us taste every day without "taste." We eat without appreciation, we fantasize without understanding, we dream without remembering, and we "make love" without loving. We are cloyed, satisfied without desire or need. We take without need, and, as a result, we do not appreciate. We are desensitized, unable to feel ecstasy or infinity. We even pray without fulfillment because we have nothing to fill. We are already satisfied. Can we who have no needs meet God? Perhaps. Maybe we are making a mistake "in the beginning." Maybe we have needs of which we are not aware.

The dissatisfaction with our life, the anxiety about our performance, the ambiguity we feel about our children, the fear that comes to us at night, the insecurity that intrudes on our quiet moments, the anger that surfaces in our work, and the competence with which we dress ourselves are hints of our need.

All of us are seekers, our question being "Where is God—meaning—sense; what is the purpose?"

The pursuit is the discovery. We cannot own God, security, meaning. We can only pursue him—it, by living. Listening to living may be the answer. It may also be the more revealing question.

The more revealing question is, "Can we find certainty in living? Can we be sure? Or can we only believe?" If the most we can achieve is belief, then faith is the answer. But faith in what? In whom? If we do not need certainty, we need not answer those questions.

MEETING
CERTAINTY

Certainty is desired. All of us would like it. The Scholastic philosophers and theologians emphasized that certainty was impossible for us. We are "contingent upon" beings, persons dependent upon an unknown providence, a direction and support over which we have no control. In the light of death, disease, and faltering human relationships most of us can agree. We can be certain about very little.

We commit ourselves to a lifetime of loving, only to find that we cannot love that long. We give ourselves to a lifetime career, only to find that careers are limited. We embrace a life of service, only to find that the service is not needed. We change. Needs change. People change. So we find ourselves in uncertainty, exactly where God or creation intended us to be. Half of the fun of living is the challenge of uncertainty.

Our spouse was not supposed to die this early. Our job was not supposed to end yet. Our profession was supposed to be more fulfilling. We didn't know it would end this way!

We can collapse in despair, persist with determination and boredom, or find new ways that appear more promising. Chances are that we do not look for certainty. We are looser. We may be happier. But we are certainly less certain. That path is attractive, but unpromising. Death and taxes are the only certainties, and neither is attractive or promising.

Still, some of us cling to certitude. We are most reluctant to let go of the old to try the new. Mostly we sit in silence and in defense. We come to experience the new only to disprove its value.

21

Coming without expectation,
  Hearing with evaluation:
    The silence of sureness

The minutes, the hours, the days
  Pass in consternation and frustration.
Each thought, each experience
  Evaluated by the past, evading explanation.
    The silence of sureness

No dreams to stir cauldron's hope,
  No risks to alter perceptions of success.
    The silence of sureness

You cannot try the new
  With a hand that firmly grips the past.
"It will not work: this new view,
  It is a passing fad that will not last!"
    The silence of sureness

The loss is mine? The loss is yours?
  Or will the balm of time dissolve
    The silence of sureness?

I wrote this poem following a workshop on experience-centered learning. The participants were veteran teachers; many had taught for twenty to thirty years. Silence was their predominant characteristic. They sought confirmation rather than information. When they presented lessons using the "new approach," they regularly fell into their lesson plans of decades of experience. Understandable and pitiful. We naturally do what we do best. We use our expertise. We fear, we avoid what we do not know. We are comfortable in a rut. Change is a challenge that most of us choose to avoid, if possible.

Not everything new is better. Not everything new needs to be tested by everyone or every profession. It is only possible that the new is better. Can we ignore it regularly? Are we willing to pay the price of "silence" in the face of doing things better? Who, then, is the one who loses? When can we stop changing

22

without doing a disservice to those whom we serve? Our silence needs to be shattered with probing questions, unfamiliar experience, and evaluation. It seems our thirst for certainty can never be slaked as long as the "new" is presented. The "new" is troublesome. It is uncomfortable. Is it promising? Only if we do not experience it will we not know the answer. The "silence of sureness" answers nothing. Risking what is new may answer something. We know what we do not have. We need to make the changes to have it. Sitting in silence and certainty maintains our deprivation.

Most of us are deprived of *something*. We lack a job, or at least the "right" job. Or we lack dignity, a healthy self-respect, peace in our lives, communication with our loved ones, security, stability, or happiness. Saint Augustine spoke for many of us when he said that our hearts are restless until we can rest in God. We finite beings seem to have an infinite thirst.

There are those who use our uncertainty and thirst for their own purposes. They tell us that we must die in order to live and, since there is something of profound truth in such a statement, we tend to accept it. We know that change requires leaving behind something, dying to an old way or love, and that our thirst for certitude and what is better promises to be quenched only by changing. But those who would use us take the profound truth of death-resurrection and try to crush us. Playing God, they pretend to know what is best for us. They do not want us to change. They have learned how to handle us as we are. They want us to stay in the job that is "not right," to accept our lack of dignity and self-respect as humility, to accept conflicts as purifying, to rejoice in our dependence on them or to let happiness wait until heaven. And we are left to murmur, "But doesn't God want us to be happy now?" What kind of God makes His creatures to be unhappy? We leave the presence of the "users" bemused and beguiled!

> The robin says spring, the gun says war.
> The child says life, the car says death.
> One chooses
> or
> One muses.

Life is ours, it belongs to each
To live, to abuse, to trample
                    or
              To reach.
We cannot call the plays,
We must obey the signals.
Our weakness is a peach
To tyrant, super salesman and sublime:
To be crushed is to live,
To die is to rise.
So, super salesman and religious,
Both can have their ways.
And we, we children who believe
              Stand bemused
                    and
                 Beguiled!

Is it all a matter of perspective? After all, the users are not always insincere or deceptive. Many are honest people. If they are different from the "used," it is in their conviction and in their own clarity of vision. We who are uncertain still struggle with a clouded vision. At least it sometimes seems so. Great leaders seem to have possessed great certitude and clarity of vision, leaders such as the great Saint Teresa, George Washington, and Pope John XXIII. But bad leaders seem equally gifted, leaders like Cardinal Richlieu, Hitler, and Jimmy Jones. Perhaps our perspective does make the difference. Much depends on what we see as real. It doesn't have to be real. We need only to see it as such.

Our perception has all of the consequences. We treat poorly those whom we perceive as insignificant. We treat well those whom we perceive as useful. We spend much time on what we perceive as important. We spend little or no time on what we perceive as unimportant. We quiet our conscience by perceiving a difference between "quality" time and "quantity" time. In fact, time is only quantity, but we choose not to perceive the reality. And there is the trap. We choose our perceptions, thereby choosing the consequences. We think we are seeing reality, when, in fact, we are constantly creating what is real for us.

Monsignor Quixote and Sancho, in Graham Greene's *Mon-*

signor Quixote, would have no trouble with our creating reality for ourselves. They felt there was a difference between the real and the imagined, but it was difficult to tell "Fact and fiction again...one can't distinguish with any certainty." Still, that might not be bad. If uncertainty can mold a lovable Monsignor Quixote, and if certainty can mold an arrogant Hitler, I for one am content to be uncertain. If we, like Descartes, need to recite "I think, therefore I am" to resolve our fuzziness, all is not lost. The world continues to turn according to its arcane laws, the planets of Scipio still play music, apples fall down and not up, and real people make love. Reality is there, and most of us continue to live as though we perceived it. It seems to make little difference whether we do or not.

"If," the creator of dreams.
    "If" I loved you like it seems,
    "If" the moon shone forth her beams
    Just to light your hair!
Would we share different dreams?

The child knows no "if."
The world he makes is real and true.
Are we, you and I, blind to what is real
Because we pretend to value what is true?

"If" horses crawled,
"If" cows had wings,
"If" trees were blue
And winds never really blew,
Would life still sing
And hope still save?

Only the "infallible" can be certain.

You and I know only what it seems to be:
    The blue sky,
    The stormy sea,
    The buzzing bee.
But "if" these are not so,
Life and truth need not be brought low.

Do values make a difference? Do values introduce us to certainty? Sometimes...maybe. Many of us might remember the meaning of a value from Raths, Harmin, and Simon: it is something freely chosen from alternatives after thoughtful consideration, cherished, admitted publicly, acted upon, and repeated.[1] Though their value clarification process was effective for me as a trainer and teacher, Raths, Harmin, and Simon's definition always seemed incomplete. I was most happy, therefore, when Brian Hall offered his definition of a value: "Any person, relationship or object which when freely chosen and acted upon contributes to the self's meaning and enhances its growth."[2] A value can help us to meet healthy certainty if it is life-giving.

If we seek healthy certitude, valuing life is a good place to start. At least, it might deter us from the arrogant certitude that may have left us bemused and beguiled. It seems to me that values come like a prayer wheel or necklace of pearls: connected. If we value life, we value love; if we value love, we value the environment of mutual respect, of mutual helping and of mutual caring that supports love's growth. In my perspective, that is all I need to be certain of, both in myself and in others. As Thomas Aquinas would say, "All the rest is straw."

Part of our pearl necklace needs those decades of discipline, fidelity, self-sacrifice, and patience, not because they are love but because they are the safeguards of love. We err, in my opinion, if we mistake the skin for the peach, the safeguard for love itself. Discipline, fidelity, self-sacrifice, and patience may not even be signs of love. They may only be ways of coping with a bad situation, a commitment regretted or a failure not admitted. Still, they deserve a place on our necklace because genuine love and life need such companions.

But who would argue against life and love as roads upon which we can meet the only certitude that is important? Even the Scriptures tells us that "God is love." (I John 4:8b) Probably only a few would oppose such "claptrap" verbally. More oppose it behaviorally. We need to be more certain of our tax returns, of our car's dependability, and of our mortgage payments than we need to meet certainty in love and life. We don't create an

---

[1]*Values and Teaching* (Columbus, Ohio: Merrill Publishing, 1966), 28-29.
[2]*The Development of Consciousness* (Ramsey, N.J.: Paulist Press, 1976), 24.

environment for growth in life and love. We do the opposite. We suspect our co-workers, our friends, our children, our wife or husband. We distrust the shopkeeper and the politician, the priest and the police officer, the mail carrier and the bus driver. We know a hundred insults, but only enough compliments to satisfy the thirst of a gnat. We are quick to attribute evil intentions and slow to applaud the "do-gooder." Perhaps our suspicions and distrust are somewhat justified; maybe we don't know how to compliment, and sometimes the "do-gooder" does more harm than good. Contrary to Leibniz, we do not live in the most perfect of worlds. But we do live in a world where there is life and love, provided we protect the environment.

Actually, I think that life and love are hardy beings, not easily killed by man or beast, by society or religion. Their roots are vital and deep, going back to that day when man and woman walked out of the jungle on two legs each. They may even reach beyond, to the love of a father for his son and the decision to make a world full of sons and daughters. We may have to go "way back" to meet love.

MEETING
LOVE

*E*ven if we must go "way back" to meet love, it is worth the trip. It is a necessary trip for most of us.

We believers like to theologize. We like to find our roots in God and in what God has told us about himself. When we relate God and love, the ground is fertile for theologizing. In a sense, God has always loved himself. He seems never to have had a problem with his self-image. The Father's knowledge and understanding of himself is so perfect that it includes the perfection of being a person. The father calls this person his Son. We call him Jesus or Christ, depending on how well we know him. But the action doesn't stop there. There is more to God than Father and Son. The Son is the perfect image of the Father. Both Father and Son know and love each other with perfection, so just as the Father's perfect understanding of himself begets the perfection of an individual personality, so does the perfect love between Father and Son give rise to the perfection of a third person, the Holy Spirit, love personified.

Now that is some trip. That's what I meant when I said that we may have to go "way back" to meet love. I find that kind of probing to be most exciting, probably because much of my academic training was in theology. It may not increase your pulse rate a bit. That's O.K.

I have a brother-in-law who is content to find love in his wife and child. He feels that he has "met it all" in them. There seems to be something to his view. We may not all have to make the long trip back to meet love. Love seems to meet us more than halfway, in parents, relatives, our spouse, or our children. Even those who know nothing of the long trip know love. We believers would say that God expresses his love for us through others. Some of us sense it as God. Others may not be sensitive to that gentle touch, but our insensitivity does not lessen the presence of the touch. Indeed, that gentle touch can be very demanding.

>Like surging waves that play
>above the surging sea,

>Like fireflies that sparkle
>in the dormant eve,

>Like hopes that linger
>in those who no longer see,

>Like visions that give faith
>when life cannot believe,

>You wander in my life,
>all moonlit dreams,

>To tell me that the world
>is what it seems:

>A world of love that strives
>to shield its heart of care,

>But, deep inside, cannot find peace
>until we share.

To meet love is to meet demands. We are caught up in storm and fury, warm breezes and cool fountains, bolts of lightning and whirling cyclones, oceans without depth and heights without limits. Song and poetry have tried to share the experience for centuries. If God is love, we can understand why love is so difficult to describe. As we reflected in the first chapter, God is unutterable and indescribable. Can love be less?

I wrote these words five days ago. Since then, I found that

I might have a second child, but it is not certain. There is danger of miscarriage. The philosophers have told us that we cannot love what we do not know. I wonder. Again my experience indicates that theory does not embrace all that it needs to embrace. The intellect is more limited than the heart.

My second child is an unknown, still buried in the throes of becoming. But I know she or he is here, on this planet, struggling for existence. I want to raise flags, to open up rivers of strength, and to create tides of life that will welcome this new being onto the shore of our planet. I want this being to know that struggle is part of the life upon which she or he has already embarked. I want this being to know that we want to applaud him or her, that we want to feel his or her arms about us, and that we want to make a fuss over him or her. I want to do all of these things for an unknown, a person I have never met. Relationships are more of the heart than of the mind.

In his book *Anatomy of Reality* Jonas Salk says, "Evolution is a process of changing relationships. . . . When good triumphs over evil, it is not for moral reasons alone, but as part of the error-correcting process of evolution." Salk seems to be closely approaching Teilhard de Chardin. Both seem to be touching the God of relationships.

The philosophers tell us that God is a necessary being: who he is he must be. Otherwise, he? she? could not be God! But what has he told us about himself (herself)? We have been told that God is a relationship of Father, Son, and Spirit—or Mother, Daughter, and Spirit. The gender is unimportant. What is important is that we are made in the image of a being whose very essence is found in relationships. He/she could not be otherwise, and neither can we. It would be more beneficial if we reflected on the importance of relationships than on the importance of gender. We shall find our potential filled in our relationships. Individual strengths, as useful as they are to relationships, are of value only insofar as they contribute to healthy, life-giving relationships. It is difficult, if not impossible, to reflect a creator whose very being is in relationships as an individual. Saints are those whose lives are entangled in life-giving ways with others. Even hermits relate to us through prayer.

Ever since the incarnation, God has said to us, "Visible support, friendship, is important. Floods, wars, and plagues may sometimes speak of me, but friendship always speaks of me." If visible relationships were unimportant, Jesus would never have been born of Mary, loved his friends, nor died so visibly for us. I once reflected on Jesus in the light of my wife:

> Who is it who conquers with gentleness?
> Who is it who supports me in my fears?
> Angels who ward off the dangers,
> Saints who show me the use of my years
> Saints and angels! My hat's off to you!
> But Kate plays a big part, too!

It seems to me that many of us go through the process of error-correction that Jonas Salk defines. For some, we find our correction in prayer and in religion. For others, it is found in our relationships. We sense that our relationships are not in tune with God's call to us. Or, if we do not believe in God, we find our relationships unfulfilling, disrupting, and painful. It may be that we are experiencing the gentle touch. The harshness we feel comes from our friends, our loves, our relationships. Behind the roughness, there could be all the gentleness of Elijah's "gentle breeze." We may only need to stand at the entrance of our cave to meet love.

But it is not easy to go to the entrace of our cave, to "error-correct," in the Salk phraseology. Relationiships can become so entangled, so complex, so confusing that we might as well try to disentangle a fishing line. We need to distinguish the "lines" that are of love and those that are not. We need to distinguish between loyalty, love, fidelity, and commitment. What is not of love needs to be cut. That is error-correction in human relationships. Loyalty, fidelity, and commitment belong only with love.

> Her hair shone bright in the Sunday sunlight
> Sparkling with truth and caring and concern—
>
> And all of it was true.

She brought life where propriety had been,
She brought joy where hurtful cynicism held its court,

And she brought love,
Where loyalty disguised as love had been.

And all of it still is.

She walks in the birthright of love,
Talks in the cadence of caring,
And shares a wondrous vision of what still can be.

Sunshine on a Sunday morning,
Shining in her hair.

Perhaps we need to error-correct our thinking that we can love only what or whom we know. God is a being of three persons. None of us has known such a being. Yet many of us profess love for him/her. We do not know the person with whom we fall in love. Ask any married couple. Yet we love him/her. To know another requires the unfolding of layer after later, the removal of veil after veil, the passage of time. Perhaps that is why heaven is forever. It will take that "time" to know an incomprehensible God. We can love an unknown person, perhaps somewhat like parents love a child who is struggling and working to "become." Knowing the other can intensify our love. Unfortunately knowing the other can also lessen our love.

All the qualities of a promise are found in meeting love. There is the quality of hope. We cannot guarantee the fulfillment of a promise. We only hope to keep it. There is the quality of limitation. We promise in the dim light of an unknown future, a future that can enhance our hope but that can also make hope's quest impossible. There is the quality of courage, the courage to try to walk straight in a world whose ways are often circular or haphazard, if not simply crooked. There is the quality of trust. We believe in the other and in ourselves, so that both of us become vulnerable and defenseless in each other's presence. In short, meeting love brings with it promises sincerely and freely

33

given, whether they are spoken or not, but we remain finite. We cannot hold back the rain nor can we raise the sun.

> Time to love—
> Time to be—
> All that we are and hope to be.
> The time of the dove.
>
> The power of God's church stood
> In mute admiration,
> Like peacocks that have viewed the rainbow.
>
> Love became incarnate,
> Truth, at last, did out,
> That all that matters is love,
> Love of self,
> Love of *the* other,
> Love of others.
>
> It is a desperate truth
> Where courts and logic are held at bay,
> Like fire in water,
> Or light in darkness.
> It is a king's room
> And a devil's nightmare.
>
> And so, the journey has begun,
> Too long left only to be sung
> And not pursued.
> The risk, the hope, the fearful dream
> That love, after all, is supreme.
>
> A time to love,
> A time to be
> All that we are and hope to be.
> The time of the dove.

For the believer meeting love is much like meeting God, as the mystics describe their encounters with him. It is an ecstasy, a movement out of oneself. It is singing simply because you are on the way to meet the loved one. I used to do that even in my days of "puppy love." Is this another indication that we are made in the image of a God of relationships? It seems so. It seems that we are not content with ourselves. We are driven out of our house, as it were, because we do not feel at home there. Perhaps we bore ourselves. Modeled on God's pattern, we have a thrust toward the other within us. Perhaps this is the real *élan vital,* the "life force" of the Belgian philosopher Bergson.

Our inner thrust lends a red violence to meeting love, causing us to risk what before was thought unriskable. Scripture scholars suggest that God himself is violent in establishing his kingdom: "The kingdom of heaven clears a way for itself by violence, and the violent are taking it by storm." (Matthew 11:12) Violence does not seem gentle at first glance. We think of war, of murder, of personal violation. But risk is always violent. It is violent to risk our life by giving it to another in love. It is violent to give birth to a baby. We are violent when we take a knife from children because we love them. This is the gentle, caring violence that accompanies love in our meeting.

The violence of love takes our attention from all except the loved one. It does not strip us of the capacity to love others as deeply and as sincerely as *the one,* but others are seen in the arms of *the one.* Maybe, because we are finite, we need such a focus. The believer finds rest and comfort in focusing on God, believing that from him all love comes. Others find themselves content with focusing on husband, wife, children, perceiving them as the real love in a world that is indifferent. To focus on *one* love does not cripple us in our need to love many. Not knowing love is the crippler.

Parents and teachers have known for years something that behavioral science has only recently articulated: that when we change a relationship with one person in our life there is a similar change in our relationships with the other people in our life. When we fall in love, everyone is dear to us. The world itself changes from drab to rosy. The sky is bluer, the ocean is more sparkling, and the flowers are brighter. Even little brother approaches the angelic. When we are upset by another, we find problems with many other people in our life. We snap, we contradict, and we snub not only the person with whom we are angry, but many others as well.

In other words, loving the one actually increases our inclination and ability to love many others. We may choose to reserve intimate sharing and making love with the one, but this only means that we can love in many different ways. It need not mean that we must love one less if we love another more. I sometimes wonder if we should not stop measuring love and just accept it. We may not be able to love God and mammon, but we can certainly love God and people. Believers have not always demonstrated this capacity. Non-believers haven't had to.

Love seems to be a specialty of children. They evoke it and they give it. It makes us childlike. Like children, we may impart magical powers to all kinds of things and to all kinds of people. We "fetishize" and adore the life we have created. Like God, we say "It is good!" Patrick, our son, is so filled with love that he wants no one and nothing to feel neglected. He waves good-bye to buildings when he leaves them. He waves good-bye and throws a kiss to my office when we close for the evening. Love gives a new respect to all creation, including what is manufactured.

People in love often give a magical quality to places and things, especially to those places where love was felt most intensely. Such places speak of love incarnate, seen, heard, and tasted. They are special.

Nantucket is such a place for me. I find that I almost identify Nantucket with my love.

> The Gray Lady rose like a spectre from the past,
>> Her spires reminiscent of dreamy country lanes
>>> and squired gardens.
>> Her cobbled streets and star studded nights held
>>> our secrets—
> But not all.
> She knew only part:
>> The part of passionate youth,
>> Of fun and love that, like a reddened sky
>>> at night,
>> Heralded a glorious tomorrow.

Like rockets contradict the night,
Like sunset makes a desert painted,
Like moonlight turns an ocean into crystal,
  She shone in splendor,
  Ready to make today yesterday,
    and yesterday tomorrow!

There is nakedness in tenderness,
And strength in defenselessness.
Not with power lies the victor,
But with love.

The dream, the hope, the fear became one.
The past, the present, the future became one.
Birth, life and rebirth became one.

The need fulfilled.
The dream completed.
Like incense on Christmas Eve,
She spoke of sweetness,
  of release,
  of newness.

It is the moon reborn,
The sun rekindled,
The heart revived.

She promised love is infinite,
And she, the ancient harlequin of faithful wife
  and honest man,
Makes no jest of the love-filled night.

Her truth lies in giving,
Her dream is for living.
It is the beginning.

Love makes special places, not only in hearts but in sands, mountains, and islands.
    Saint Paul tried to describe the meeting of love, but he could

only say what it was not. It is not a lot of noise, such as "a cymbal clashing." It is not knowledge or prophecy. It is not faith, even "faith in all its fullness, to move mountains." It is not generosity or martyrdom. He did say love is patient, kind, never jealous, never boastful, never conceited, never rude or selfish. Love does not take offense, nor is it resentful. Love takes no pleasure in the failure of others. ". . . it is always ready to excuse, to trust, to hope, and to endure whatever comes. Love does not come to an end." (See I Corinthians 13:1–8)

Paul speaks of the love of "agapé," the Greek word for selfless love. The Greeks contrasted "agapé" with "eros," love that was predominantly self-seeking. The contrast, of course, is not complete, for there is always something of self-seeking in all love. The philosophers used to tell us that we respond only to that which appears "good" to us. Good is the natural goal of the will. What does not appeal to us, what does not seem good to us, does not attract us. Love is as fulfilling, as tenuous, as difficult, as demanding as it might prove to be. In the end, if we meet love, it is lasting. We may "fall out of love," but we shall seek it again. Love makes us whole. We want to be complete, no matter the cost. We share that need with God. It is kind of a divine selfishness.

MEETING
JOY

*J*oy is a meeting of spirits, a coming together of those who have a common feeling, a common love, or a common vision. When the "commonality" is celebrated, there is joy. It is not common. It is not frequently experienced.

Lust is not joy. Celebration is not joy. Sharing victory is not joy. Success is not joy. Making love is not joy. Shedding problems is not joy. Finding aloneness is not joy. Having money is not joy. Being a member of a family is not joy. Being a member of a community is not joy. Being anything or anyone is not joy. Joy comes only in unison with others.

We can celebrate, share a victory, make love, solve problems, be a member of a family or of a community and not find joy. Joy is a communal event. We cannot find it without others being equally involved. To think that we can find it in isolation is a delusion. To think that we shall find it in association with others is also a delusion.

Joy is a happening, the meeting of kindred spirits. The meeting may be short or long, over dinner, a drink, or over a lifetime. It may be analyzed or simply accepted, recognized or simply enjoyed. In the end, we may only know that it happened, that we *had* it. As we reflect, we recognize some different experience. And we liked it.

> They were happy, they were real.
> People, real people in love with life.
> That was yesterday.
> Today, the sun shone, the birds sang,

39

And they returned,
Better for having been themselves.
A night of fun and reverie,
A night the Lord himself had made.

Never forget the "Child,"
Never forget the "Child,"
That strains in each of us to give birth
    to joy and abandon.

If thou wouldst be shamed,
Be shamed by "Parent"
Who would dull your powers
    and
Make empty your fullness.

Transactional Analysis has contributed to us the vocabulary of joy and restraint. Our "Parent" nurtures us, cares for us, allows us to care for ourselves, and is necessary to us. Once we lose our parents by death or by distance, we need to have a Parent in our own head. The Parent tells us that we are significant, that we are loved and that there are limits. We are significant and important, but we need to be disciplined.

Our "Child" drives us to enjoy, to have fun, and to test limitations. Joy is seated in the Child. Unrestrained, the Child will destroy us. Guided by the Parent, the Child may be muted or supported. Left to itself, the Child may become wild, without joy or real satisfaction. The Child in each of us seeks personal satisfaction. It seeks to please. It seeks to create, to make relationships we have never thought of before. It seeks individuality, recognition and lovability. The Child is not a memory, a recalling of what it was like to be cuddled, cared for, and protected. Our Child *IS* a reality for us when we choose to give it freedom. We *are* five years old again. We are helpless, dependent, and loving. Transactional Analysis suggests such a reality. I endorse it. I believe it is so. In this sense, we differ from the Freudian theories that emphasize the effects of childhood experiences upon our present behavior. When we are motivated as children, when we act as children, we *are* children. The Child remains present in all of us.

40

Thank God it does, for only in a Child to Child relationship can we find intimacy and joy. If we relate Parent to Parent we are protective, solicitous, and understanding. We might even be censuring. If we relate Adult to Adult we share information, facts, figures, and statistics. Joy is an experience of closeness, of intimacy and vulnerability that belongs to the child part of our personality. Guards are discarded, protections are set aside and fences are lowered. Parents and Adults won't allow this to happen. They need control.

Our Child opens the gates of defensiveness. We allow another to see us as we are. Our energies are not diverted to protecting ourselves. All of our effort is reaching out to the other. And joy needs the other. We cannot find joy by ourselves, perhaps because we are made in the image of a God whose joy is found in his Son and in his Spirit. Like God, we can find fulfillment only in the kindred spirit, in the other who reflects ourselves. Perhaps that is a kind of selfishness. If it is, so also is God selfish!

The other may not be our mirror image. The other might even be our opposite. It is only important that the other be fulfilling, that the other seem good to us. By nature, we cannot be drawn to what is not good for us. Our will is attracted only to the "good." We have no appetite for what we perceive as harmful, evil, or distasteful. This has nothing to do with morality. It has everything to do with behavior and motivation. We are attracted to what and to whom we like. Observe a child for a short time. You will see what I mean.

But children are sometimes drawn to what is harmful to them. That is the risk of intimacy. What we perceive as good may not be good. Our thrust toward intimacy carries the risk of hurt. We become vulnerable. Seeking joy, we find pain. Still, it is worth the risk.

> It was a long road
>   That seemed so short.
> Like Genesis, there first was nothing.
> The power sat powerless,
> The knowledgeable were silent.
>   It was a time to act,

41

And there was silence.
Then, like a mighty finger,
   The Spirit stirred the mass.
First, there was chaos,
   Then doubt, then interest, then hope,
   And finally enthusiasm and esprit!

For a while Camelot and Eden
   Wrestled to possess the day.
Hope, will and clarity
   Cut open the fog of stupefaction
   And showed tomorrow's sun.
There was joy
   and dancing
      and tranquillity.

What happened?
Why did it stop?

Or has it stopped?

Is the glimmer glinting still today self born?
Are new-born infants without ancestoring?
Has it ceased to be?
Or have we ceased to see?

What we have borne in joy may not always be possessed
in joy. Yet, what is borne in joy never ceases to be. We may be
blind to its life. We may not recognize our offspring. We may
feel failure. But being borne of joy assures immortality.

Joy can't be expressed in prose. It can only be celebrated
in poetry. It is a meeting, a joining, a moment of sharing that
happens rarely. The sharing might continue for weeks, for
months or for years, but it still seems short-lived and temporary.
It is difficult to maintain joy. Its moment is *now*.

We celebrated the end and the beginning.
The January sea was like July,
Cavorting and leaping in salty sprays of nostalgia.

Poinsettias bloomed in ever widening expanses,
Bespeaking life, and beauty and God!

Only friendship grew taller than sea and poinsettia.

It was a time of trust,
   a time of freedom,
   a time of joy,
When family embraced the stranger,
When "faith" exposed God's glory to man and woman,
When dreams were felt to be lived,
And hopes became enfleshed.

When we experience joy we meet the old and the new. There is a strange joining of what was meaningful and what is meaningful. It is a kaleidescope of life when life is worth living. The past and present become one; they promise an unlimited future of fulfilled dreams and incarnated fantasies. Joy is not ecstasy. It is *esprit*, the Spirit whispering, cavorting, and being the Spirit.

There is a timeliness to joy. When we have experienced it, we continue to live with it. In this sense it is mystical. Failures, difficulties, ugliness cannot destroy what we have experienced. It is a testimony to the goodness of life, an act of faith in the reality of the incarnation, an experience of the unity and love of humankind. It is an affirmation of life.

Where there is no joy, there is death in its final form. If we have never experienced joy, we cannot experience life. We may take refuge in our faith in an afterlife, our belief that we are not meant to be joyful here, in this world. We may take consolation in the reality of a heaven where joy will be eternal. But the seed has limitations. The rose cannot grow from crabgrass, nor the lily from swedish ivy. What we are not here, we cannot be eternally. God created us to reflect himself, his love of life, his love of creation. He saw all of creation as good, a source of joy, of consolation, of exaltation. If we do not experience his view, death is not violent enough to change us. We shall not experience hereafter what we do not appreciate here. Life hereafter is a continuance of what we are. Our task is to grow to heaven. We are not meant

43

to be carried there against our will and perceptions.

The gentleness of God carries us from where we are to where we are. He is not a transport. We use the time of this life to grow as we choose. Death does not escalate that transformation. It only changes the kind of life we experience. Death does not violate. It transforms.

Joy unknown here is joy unknown in heaven. We do not please God with sacrifices of food and flesh. He is a God of joy, a God who created us for exhilaration in our productivity and achievement, a God who triumphs with our triumphs, a God who shares human success with us.

What are your endless sacrifices to me?
...Bring me your worthless offerings no more,
the smoke of them fills me with disgust.
...Take your wrong-doing out of my sight.
Cease to do evil.
Learn to do good,
search for justice,
help the oppressed,
be just to the orphan,
plead for the widow. (Isaiah 1:13–17)

I once had a supervisor who did not believe in any hereafter. Her conviction was that if we were to do good, it had to be here and now. For her, the hereafter was a cop-out. It dispensed us from doing all that we could *now* to better the world and its people.

Her conviction has haunted me. We Christians have been encouraged to suffer self-imposed penances, to subject ourselves to sacrifices and to "offer up" indignities for the sake of the kingdom and for our own salvation. But can we accept a God who wants us to live so? Perhaps. Perhaps we have been so corrupted by original sin that we need to gain heaven by this kind of violence.

Original sin seems to militate against joy. Our suspicion is that if we enjoy "it," "it" must be wrong. Both joy and sin are

44

concerned with goals or "ends." As rational beings, we are strongly influenced by purpose. "So what?" is our question. "Why are we doing what we are doing?" Original sin seems to make all of our natural actions evil.

Richard of Middleton, a Franciscan commentator on St. Thomas Aquinas, suggests that original sin does nothing to harm our faculties of intellect and will. We understand and choose as well as we ever could. It is our goal that is disrupted by sin; our target is off course. Had God not given us a goal of faith and grace, we would have had a natural goal of being all that we could be. Once we deserted God's goal of life with him, we were left with our goal of personal fulfillment. The problem for the believer is that there is not, nor ever has been, personal fulfillment without life in God. We are not what we seem to be. We are part of the divine family. We stand confused, disoriented, and joyless. We seek in sin what we can find only in divinity. We suspect all joy. Meeting joy creates confusion. We feel guilty. Piet Schoonenberg in *Man and Sin* supports this observation. We are whole. Joy is legitimate. But, we need to refocus our target.

If we can find our target, if we can orient our goal to what is sympathetic to our real self, we can meet joy. We find it at the end of the dark path through self, in the light that glows after false experience and in the healthy dream we have made come true.

Joy is an exaltation in what we are and in what we can be. Taking pleasure in ourselves and in our loved ones is joy. It is being content with our limitations, while we are secure in our effort to surpass them. We cannot be joyful and insecure. Then we are too dependent. We take joy in another but not in ourselves. We need to feel *worthy* to feel joy.

If we feel joy and do not feel worthy, we feel guilt. Guilt can be healthy, a recognition that we have done wrong. Guilt indicates a conscience, a faculty within us that distinguishes moral good from moral evil. It tells us that we have not "hit the target" of divinity, that we have missed the truth of who we are, why we are here and what our purpose is. Guilt tells us that we know there is more to living than living, that life is more than a series of episodes, birth, growth, marriage, childbearing, loving, child caring, and senior citizenship.

When we are children we need boundaries, artificially set by our parents. Growth and maturity do not lessen the need for boundaries. Guilt supplies the need. We know that we are for a purpose, that we need to fulfill responsibilities and that conscious rejection of our purpose and responsibilities is unacceptable. Believer or not, we can feel guilt. The believer has the advantage of labeling guilt as a transgression of moral principles and of having ways to diffuse the guilt: confession and expiation. Unbelievers are left to their own devices. In either case, we are inclined to repair the damage done, insofar as we are able. The point is that guilt makes us accountable for our actions.

If we are too immersed in our own unworthiness, if we experience life as an undeserved gift or if we perceive ourselves as unfit or unworthy, it is most difficult to experience joy without remorse. If we are not supposed to be happy, then it is sinful to be happy. Meeting joy is a disturbing experience.

Preliminary to joy is the conviction that we are significant, that we are loved and that life is meant to be enjoyed rather than endured. We need to accept our creation in the image of God whose very essence is joy, the possession of what is fulfilling. We are never closer to the fulness of our creation than when we are joyous. Then we reflect who we are and what we are more clearly than at any other time. Human beings are optimists. The pessimist is the square peg trying to fit into the round hole.

God made us to have what we need. He gave us the world to fill our needs. He is insulted by depression, sadness, and misery. He is reflected in joy, exaltation, and happiness. Through Jesus God told us that he is found where there is love: ". . .love one another, as I have loved you. I have told you this so that my own joy may be in you and your joy may be complete." (John 15:12, 11)

Like meeting love, to meet joy is to meet God. We may not believe in God, but we shall know that we have a purpose and a reason for being. Joy is the mirror in which we see our full selves and our reason for existence. We find joy with others.

But what of aloneness? Did not God also create that? Was it not his first thought in the story of Genesis? Only when he saw man as lonely did he rethink his plan: "It is not good that man should be alone. I will make him a helpmate." (Genesis 2:18) It seems to me that God was not completely successful in his effort to overcome loneliness. We still meet it. We still need to deal with it. It can be an experience of joy, but more often it is not.

MEETING
LONELINESS

Many of us create our own loneliness. At first we are like part of a marble quarry, whole and entire with our environment. There comes along a person, a cause, a job that offers more. We are attracted. We accept. We succumb. We chip off part of ourselves, our friends, and our relationships, because the position demands it. We allow others to chip off their bits from us, making us what we are "supposed" to be. Like the *Pietá,* we stand stripped of what God created around us. We may be beautiful, but lonely. We serve others, but not ourselves.

Perhaps only God should find us in the essence of what we are, since only he, it seems, can fill vacuums. When we allow others to strip us, to change us, to eliminate our excess growth, we submit ourselves to those who cannot replace loss. These others cannot be with us always, nor do they intend to be. They can only challenge us to rebuild, to grow, and to refurnish. They mean well. But they can make us lonely. Perhaps they are God's instruments, challenging us to be all that he intended us to be. Still, it can be a lonely journey, as worthwhile as it can be. If we can make "connections," if we can find those who fill our loneliness, the journey is worthwhile. Fundamentally, the journey out of loneliness is a lonely journey.

To be *alone* can be joyous. We may need to be solitary. We may have had our "fill" of others, of demands, and of expectations. For a while, we enjoy being alone. *Loneliness* is different because it carries with it a feeling of unfulfillment and of deprivation. We need not be alone to be lonely. We can be lonely surrounded by friends. Aloneness is a physical state. Loneliness is a psychological experience.

Years ago I met a physician, a gynecologist/obstetrician, at a bar in the Bahamas. He was washed out, "burned out" in current terminology. He had had enough of bodies, problems, and women. He had had enough of "being needed" and of "being important." He needed to be alone. There are such times. It is important that we choose them, that we recognize them. I have met surgeons and priests with the same need. Aloneness is not always negative. Eventually, most of us feel the need for the other, since we are made in the image of a relational God. Few of us can grow to our full potential alone.

Aloneness can be negative. We can move through our life cutting ties, avoiding intimacies in our "busyness," and "moving ahead" at the cost of relations and friends. We can move so far ahead that we find no one around. We are lonely in our success, surrounded only by those who hope to gain from our relationship. When we have moved so far, we have some experience of hell.

Jesus described hell as "fire." (Matthew 5:22b) Fire is a lonely experience. We experience it alone. I have always thought that hell is being alone, no one sharing our misery, no one in sight, no one to speak with, no one at all. That is hell. The lonely catch a glimpse of hell. All of us have done so, at one time or another. Friendship, marriage, love do not protect us. That is God's mercy. He wants us to know what the final denial of who we are and in whose image we are made will lead to. Loneliness is the final contradiction of being human, of being God's child, of a being created in the image of God. Loneliness is the antimatter, the black hole of the universe. It swallows us up, reverses us, dissolves us, and contradicts our existence.

We need it, but rarely—and never as a way of life. It happens to all of us, but we need not endure it. We need to be assured that loneliness is only temporary. We need to endure it. It best not be nurtured.

> The vibrations, the forces, the fears and dreams
> So noisy in my heart
> Are wrapped in silence before your gaze.
> Are you the same?

50

Do the noisiness and busyness
   that pound within your heart and mind
Stand mute and silent to my ear?

Even the spheres have hearers,
   We are told,
Holy devotees who have caught
   the music of their motion.

The mindless ocean,
The empty air
Speak with tongues we can write and share.

The trees are heard by the poet,
The mountain calls the adventurer.
Is man alone in all this world
Unheard in his loneliness?

    Many years ago when the liturgical movement was dawning there developed a militant group whose sole purpose in life seemed to be to convince us that community was as important to our life as the air we breathed. I felt that they would suffocate us if that would convince us. At this time of my life I no longer dispute their obsession. At that time I kept thinking that in the end there is no community. Each of us meets God alone.

    In a sense I may have been correct. Because we are finite we share in a limited way. There is a core of our being we never share because we never know it. Only God has perfect self-knowledge. Our efforts for community can never be totally successful. We can only approach the perfect community of Father, Son, and Spirit. But that is better than being alone.

    The closeness with another that abates loneliness is never complete. In a strange way each of us remains locked within ourselves. Communication is always partial. Intimacy is always limited. Unity is only an illusion, but an important illusion. We need to believe that we are one in mind and heart. The depth of our need is revealed when a "slip" uncovers our misunderstanding of the other. We feel hurt, disappointed, and betrayed. We see the one we love for the first time. We thought we knew him or her perfectly—an illusion! With this we need to be content. It is all we have.

> His retinue sailed before him
>   Like knights of old!
> "He's very honest. He'll confront you."
> Was their bold and joyous prologue.
>
> And so he came,
> A seeker like the rest of us, asking
>   "Who am I? Why am I?"
> He fitted.
>
> Together, yet alone, we sought life's meaning,
> Struggling to learn to help,
>   To help others,
> While we helped ourselves.
>
> In spite of all our oneness
>   It was a lonely journey,
>   Each beginning and ending to his own accord.
>
> Has God's spirit led us so?
> I, at least, am proud enough to answer "yes."
>   But only time and our final destiny
>   Will be believed.

For all its limitations, friendship remains for us the only rescue from loneliness. Even the love between Jonathan and David was limited.

Sometime-loneliness can be healing and life-giving. It is the stage for reflecting on the plaguing ambiguities of our lives, for taking stock, and for asking the right questions. Sometimes it can even give right answers to the right questions. Sometime-loneliness can give us perspective, take away our confusion and lead us to new strength. But even sometime-loneliness can be painful, especially when it asks the right questions for which we have no answers. One writer has described this kind of loneliness by saying that it is always 4 a.m. in the depths of the soul: that dark hour that allows those significant, answerless questions to buzz within our newly awakened head.

How many hours 'til Dawn?
As long as you make them?
As long as others allow?

Such questions plague us in the early hours,
Early hours of near despair and regretted errors.

They are the questions of the "fearing failure,"
The questions of the thoughtless route, now regretted.

Still they are valid,
Still requiring answers.

How many hours are there 'til Dawn?

Some of us seem to grow in apparent loneliness. They are the hermits and monks of the world. They may or may not be in hermitages or monasteries. I believe they are few because they have heard a "different drummer." Their needs are not like ours or, if they are, they have the conviction that the needs of solitude are more important. They place solitude, silence, mystical experience with God, mystical communion with the universe, with some supreme part of themselves or nature above the needs for friendships and relationships. Most of us find this path a dead end. There is nothing.

Still, this life may be right *for them*. Often, they are the first to admit that the lonely life is not for everyone.

On the other hand, the monks and hermits of the world may be wrong. They may share in the cynicism of the philosopher quoted by Thomas á Kempis in *The Imitation of Christ* who wrote, "As often as I have been amongst men, I have returned less a man" (Book I, Chapter XX). Aquinas stated in his essay *On Being and Essence* that a small mistake in the beginning is a large one in the end. Monks and hermits who, in their youth, followed the cynical dictum of á Kempis's philosopher may have made a "mistake in the beginning" and, in time, found themselves trapped by it. It is not good for us to be alone.

Still, those who have chosen aloneness may tell us that theirs is not the lonely life. God, nature, the muses, and the life of the intellect are their companions. They only appear to be solitary. There is no reason for us not to believe them.

The experience of loneliness is painful because we sense something of death about it. We are deprived of friends and loved ones. The solution to loneliness should be simple. Made to be with the other, we need only meet the other. Children and the innocent do find it simple to meet the other. They are not yet aware of the risks entailed. But the risks are great because the rewards are great. Risk and reward make meeting each other one of our most exciting experiences.

MEETING
EACH OTHER

*A*s painful as loneliness can be there is a certain security about
it. It carries with it the illusion of control. Perhaps that is why
some choose to remain lonely: they need not risk meeting
another. In meeting each other there is a risk. If I meet you in
sincerity, I become vulnerable to you. The deeper our meeting,
the more vulnerable I become. If I don't meet you, if you don't
meet me, you cannot hurt me. It is in knowing another that we
can hurt the other. The deepest cuts are made by genuine lovers.

She was confused and so was I,
A not unusual experience for us both.
To bridge the gap of human person,
The communication of man to woman,
            of man to man,
            of woman to man
Is to risk too much.

We fight it, belittle it, deny it;
We do not want it
Because you might change me,
            touch me,
            challenge me.

But without you there is no growth.
We stand before the court of life
  Resplendent in our eighth-grade values,
  Blessed by our crippled experiences
  And confirmed by those too scared to make choices.

"We are His chosen," says
  —our life style
  —our open commitment
  —our vocal protestations.
But we are only our own,
Seeking not to be disturbed,
  not to lose what we have,
For never might we recover
  So much again!

We are afraid.

    Only our deep need of others gives us the courage to meet another. Our need, imprinted as firmly as God's image in us, is greater than our fear.
    Our fear is manufactured out of our life experience: the hurt we remember, the unexpected insults we still feel twisting within us, the disappointments we wish we could forget. A child has not had time to be hurt so deeply. He is not afraid to meet another. Only we grown-ups are afraid. Only we remember "the other time!"
    Because our need for others is God-given, it can harness our fear. But harnessed or not, the fear remains. Perhaps it is not to be driven out in this life. Heaven is fearless communication with the other. Here, we hang between heaven and hell, never fully meeting each other and never fully alone. We are "mugwumps," our face feeling the sunshine of heaven in the warmth of friendship and our "wump" feeling the iciness of hell in the cold fear of loss or rejection. Jesus has taught us to love others. Experience has taught us to fear. But Jesus is bigger.
    Our fear takes many shapes. We may fear ourselves, distrusting our ability to share or afraid that we shall share too much. We fear that we shall be used (again) and that not enough of us will be left to live again. We fear rejection, so we wear masks believing that the mask can be rejected while we hide in a corner safe and "whole." If the other truly meets us we fear that we won't be liked, and that is all that any of us want. We want to be liked for ourselves.
    There are, of course, "people-eaters," and we don't want

them to meet us. Our fear is justified.

Still, if we are not to remain dwarfs in mind and heart, we need to risk the meeting, even with "people-eaters." We believe there is hope for everyone. Only the dead are hopeless. We need to risk being "eaten." "People-eaters" often need us more than anyone.

Sometimes we need to be "eaten," to feel the cares, concerns and burdens of others. The alternative is loneliness, personal isolation that masquerades as freedom. It is not bad to be "eaten" in that way. Other ways hurt a lot more: to be used and discarded, to be abused and ridiculed, to be belittled and discounted, to be judged, sentenced, and executed from afar. To be "eaten" by the cares of those we serve (and love?) can be life-giving.

> Are we so dull and uninspiring,
> Grey and brown like Fall's landscape,
> That mystified eyes and creaseless
>   Faces look empty and bored
> Before the fullness that we have?
>
> Has life and dream so long
>   Departed our experience
> That we cannot recall
>   The thrill of joined hands and hearts?
>
> Don't leave us unencumbered
>   With your cares and needs.
> Climb on our backs with wants and claims.
>
> In your belief
>   We'll find what we need most.
> For you believe and hope
> Far more than most,
> Far more than *we!*

All of us are half-people. The lyricist has written of our incompleteness since the first love song was sung. We long to meet the other, our second half that makes us a whole. We see only half of reality and yearn to see the whole; we dream only half a dream and thirst for its completion; we love with only half a heart until our love is returned by the other.

If our need for the other were less, the risk of meeting the other would be less. But our need is great. We need to be accepted for what we are. We need to be seen naked by the other and to be embraced, warts, scars, and all. We need to be loved. So great is the need that we spend a life in its pursuit, always hoping that the meeting will be more complete. We work to tear down *all* boundaries and walls, to experience the ecstasy in which we flow completely into the other and they into us.

Here is the life force, the *élan vital* that flees death and drives for survival. This is the power that screams "hope!" in a nuclear age. It is silenced only when our hearts become pumps, our blood a mixture of chemicals, and our brain a computer. Only machines, robots whose only trace of humanity remains in the human shape, can kill the other. So long as we cling to our humanity we feel the need to cling to the other. Full life is our destiny. The suicide and the murderer have first to let go of their humanity.

To meet another requires the "leap of faith," not of religious faith necessarily but the human faith that trusts another without any reason and without evidence. We relinquish some of our control, allowing another to lead us by the hand in a direction unknown to us. We trust ourselves to another.

For awhile we may not want to take the bother of meeting another. We can drown our sensibilities in an ocean of activity. We can turn our hearts into pumps and our brains into computers — for awhile. We can pretend to be "brains-on-stilts" and we may even convince ourselves that we are realists. We can deny our unique endowment in the animal kingdom: our self-conscious awareness of our own feelings. But it must cost us.

The "while" passes and we sense futility biting our heels. We fight it, pointing to our work, to our money, and to the respect with which we are treated. We rationalize that we are strong and others are weak. They are not worth our time or attention. We are special. We surround ourselves with "things" that proclaim our value, our brilliance, or our popularity. But all the time our armored suit of isolation becomes thicker. Anxiety and dissatisfaction won't go away. Something is missing.

But some*thing* isn't missing. Some*one* is missing. The some-
one with whom to celebrate, to cry, to struggle is missing. We
may work valiantly to convince ourselves we are happy. Like a
wrestler we sit with our full weight upon the need to meet the
other, certain we can subdue the need and win the match.

The match, however, is fixed. We cannot win, if to win
means to be happy. To subdue our need for the other is to harden
and to atrophy, to survive with cynicism and bitterness, to die
without burial. So, if we win, we lose.

Only if we lose do we win. To risk meeting another may
end in disappointment and distress. But we have no choice but to
take the risk. To live, to be vital, the risk is as necessary as breathing
with healthy lungs. Even by breathing we risk pollutants that can
sicken and kill. Our deepest human drives demand that we risk,
that we trust and, hopefully, that we succeed in a life-giving
meeting. If we are lucky enough to meet the right other, if we
are wise enough to meet without guile, if we are perceptive
enough to distinguish acqaintance from friend and friend from
lover we may succeed.

What is the question?
"Can friends be lovers?"
"Can lovers be friends?"

Angels know no such question.
Birds, trees and flowers need solve
    No such riddle.
Only man and woman, standing in the
    Midst of God's creation
    In solitary splendor
    Need to know.

You and I, we need to know
How true friendship is true love,
How true love is true friendship.
For friendship that is not love
    Is a mask for deceit.
And love that is not friendship
    Is brutal.

The first is but a play,
  Fit only for tragedy.
The second feeds upon the "friend,"
  Leaving behind only the husk.

Indeed, there are no answers
  To questions that do not exist,
Questions that betray our quest
To set limits where infinity belongs.

To meet the other is complex. A net is made of a number of strands that are carefully interrelated. Each strand needs to be located perfectly if the net is to function well. It is the composition of nothing, the open spaces, with something. Meeting another is no less complex.

My drives, my needs, my hopes, my dreams, my energies need to meet your drives, your needs, your hopes, your dreams, your energies like the strands of a net meet to make the whole. Then, I meet you. What we have seems to be nothing made out of something, that evanescent "thing" called friendship or love or knowing the other. The strands do not make our meeting any more than the strands make the net. It is the emptiness between the strands that make a net. Friendship and love, like the net's empty spaces, declare a meeting has happened.

Where our strands are poorly related we have tears and holes, the loss of that "nothing" that is our meeting. We may make repairs, but rarely do we re-create the same net. Which does not mean we have a poorer net. It might be better, stronger, and more buoyant.

Can we distinguish between friendship and love? The philosopher would ask "Is there a real distinction?" There are levels of friendship. There are levels of love. But can we have a friend we do not love to some degree? Can we have a love who is not a friend to some degree? Some questions, such as these, should never need to be asked. But ours is not a perfect world.

In our thirst for meeting the other we sometimes confuse friendship with the deeper expectations of the lover. We love without seeing the beloved as a friend. We confuse the behavior of love with the reality of love. We take kindness and consideration for friendship, and sometimes for love. Our need drives us to see what isn't there. It is the teenage pitfall out of which so many never grow. Never having known the face of true friendship, we find it hard to recognize. Never having experienced true love, we imagine it to be what it is not. We see friendship and love as twins. They may be sisters, but they are not twins. While they should not be confused, where we have one her sister is not far behind.

Meeting God does not always fill our need to meet another. God is not meant to fill all our human needs. He created man and woman to do that. The dark night of the soul is the struggle to fit a round God into a square slot. Eventually the slot has to be rounded, the need has to be changed. Then we have those saints whom Jesus said "could take it." We do a disservice to convince others that "it" is for everyone.

Human nature is varied enough and individualized enough to allow for saints and sinners. The constant elements of our nature are the needs and demands we feel: the need to be loved, the need to be accepted, the need to be acknowledged by others. *How* we meet those needs is not constant. We can meet them through loving relationships, through chosen isolation, or through violence. But to meet our needs without meeting the other is to do ourself violence and to pay a price. For some of us "the price is right." For most of us the price, like the price for being a hermit, is too high.

MEETING FORCE

*F*orce is part of our lives. It is a power to move us, a drive to change us, a need to be filled. Without force we vegetate, sitting immobile, waiting for the undertaker. While we do not starve to death, some of us live lives that simply do wait for the undertaker. Our dreams have long been forgotten. Our force has been weakened. Our appetite for life has been lost. We are satisfied too easily.

Still others of us are driven. Our force is overpowering, making us whirling dervishes before the altar of activity. We need to take work home, we need to see the latest movies, we need to join the Rotary Club and the Kiwanis. We need, we need, we need. We may say, "We live life to the fullest." In reality, we are like a steak eater who swallows each piece unchewed, leaving our taste buds unsatisfied. Our force is great because our needs never get time to be filled. So, we move on, always living in the future, rarely exulting in the present. We are among those who don't "Take time to smell the flowers."

Being alive is neither "busyness" nor lethargy. Life is joy, joy in being with others, joy in work, joy in play, and joy in the present. We learn from the past and anticipate the future, but we enjoy the present. *Now* is our only real possession. We need a force to be present in the present. That's easy for some of us, but not for all.

Outside forces get in our way. The family expects "this," the boss wants "that," and our friends demand something else. Our culture says that we must work ten hours a day to live in dignity. We worry about the past and fret about the future. "How

can we send the kids to college?" "How can we get a new car?"
"How can we make up for the fight with our wife (husband) last
night?" No wonder the present gets lost. It is like a small child
in the Times Square crowd on New Year's Eve. We don't notice
the child. We are so busy looking up and looking ahead that we
do not notice the newly arrived child in front of us. The present
is too fleeting to notice. There is something more interesting
ahead. We turn our head and turn back to find the child grown.
"Did we have a baby once?"

Time is a tyrant, growing in strength with the passing years.
My sons are not yet five. Sometimes I think that one day for them
is a week for me. The train gains speed at the height of the
journey. Slower speeds can be expected towards the journey's
end.

Values create force. The value of money creates forces of
work, of manipulation, or even of corruption. The value of life
creates forces of children, of marriage, and of play. The value of
freedom creates forces of war, of separation, and of self-
knowledge. The value of independence creates forces of creativity,
of separateness and, sometimes, of loneliness.

Labor camps, the Gulag Archipelago, are forces nurtured
in the value of the state. Values of institutions can create death-
dealing forces, sometimes with the best of intentions.

Crowded platforms,
  Seas of overcoats, jeans and dresses
Joining, giving, hoping in shared confusion,
  Hoping to survive the night,
  The journey, each other.

The cars were crowded
  On the way to Labor.
Men were cheap,
The State important.

Do we do less
  In our "free" institutions,
  Businesses and churches?

Pretending what is forced is free,
  What is taken has been given,
  What we have is what we want?
Do we?

What of those who will not trail this drummer?
Those who try but find such freedom wanting?
Especially those who almost lose their souls
But wake in time to bare the masquerade?

Theirs is the twilight of accomplishment,
  The "almost" of nothing.
For them the picture has turned grey and motley,
  A poison fatal to the buyer.

But in the heart that knows love and freedom,
Where dreams have been allowed to search for what is real,
The "almost" is fulfillment,
The chase has been the goal.

How we perceive a force determines its power. *We* make it powerful or weak. Perhaps we rationalize, saying that the race is more important than crossing the finish line first. Still, we have weakened the force, at least for ourselves. We choose what shapes us, drives us, makes us what we are. Therein lies the secret of meeting force and of defeating it, if we want to. We are the most powerful force in our lives.

    You people—

      You can have my best
      If that's what you expect.

    You people—

      You shall get my worst
      If you speak your worst.

      I am the master of my destiny
      Whether you exist or not.

So, dream good dreams you want of me
And give your heart in empathy.
There's little I won't give to you,
And much that I will share with you,
If only you will feel with me.

The force we let into our lives needs to be life-giving, in league with the creative thrust for growth and for development. We need to use it actively. Even healthy forces, submitted to passively, can crunch us like so many vises. Good shackles are no less shackles. Our choice of force, be it child, wife, or job is like our choice of a road. It will lead to our destination or we shall find ourselves lost. We need to choose. Few of us *happen* to get where we want to go.

We feel a force most when it is not of our choosing. It surprises us, surfacing out of a deliberate choice whose consequences we did not clearly foresee. It is like a roadblock we come upon without warning. And we may have travelled too far to go back, so we must deal with it. Rarely are these surprises pleasant.

But they can be. We find a goal more easily achieved than anticipated because unforeseen help *happens* to appear. We do a task more easily because it is not as complex as expected. These are the gentle touches that "fill the valleys and lay low the mountains." It happens.

Usually, we expect the worst. That's strange for creatures born to be happy. We keep expecting the worst even though it never happens. Perhaps we don't believe that we were born to be fulfilled, happy, and content. Maybe our doubts and our dire forecasts are some of the effects of original sin. When you've made one wrong turn you have every right to expect another.

I keep wanting to write "May the force be with you," but I'm afraid that is trite to say. Its overtones are "good against evil" and "white against black." It is superficial, bordering on comedy. Nevertheless, we need to have the force with us. If we must have force in our lives, if there is no life without force, it had better be a wind behind us, speeding us to port, than a gale at our bow.

Sometimes we use force on ourselves, we manufacture pretense, forcing ourselves to be and to feel what we neither are nor feel. We behave caring and really believe that we care. We look interested and really believe we are interested. Concern wells in our eyes and we think our heart is on fire. With force we find it easy to learn.

> Love, bottled and stoppered,
>   Enclosed in glass.
> It's done in meetings and in discussions
> With fevered brow and earnest look.
> Composed by lovers who have not loved,
> Proclaimed by priests of love
>   With only dreams to draw on.

> The illusion is the Master,
> The hope the Father.

> They mean the real,
>   And dream what all men hope:
> That what is real and needed
>   Is what I can do.

> But there is no substance in these earnest ones,
> There is no love in whom such love comes easy.
> They try so hard
>   For so little,
>   And
>   Only so long.

Pretense lasts as long as we have our way, as long as others act like we think they should act. When we are asked to give that dearest of gifts, allowing others to be themselves and accepting others for themselves, the pretense ends. We force the new pretense of pity, sorrow, or indignation. "After all I've done for you!" "Poor _____! He or she is so confused. It's a pity."

Hypocrisy is a force from within us. If our pretense with others can be likened to masks that we wear, hypocrisy is like our soul's mask. We think we are sincere. We think we are open, flexible, and loving. We are convinced. We cannot understand why others would tell us differently. We are anesthetized, forcing ourselves to see ourselves as we want to be, because then we might be able to live with ourselves. We don't want the anesthesia to wear off and have to feel the pain of what we are.

So used to force are we that we hardly ever expect the best. We expect others to want to change us. "Do you remember what you did last year?" "Why? Did I do something wrong?" We are startled to hear "No, of course not. I was thinking of how you visited me every day when I was laid up. I really appreciated that!" Then we get embarassed. How do we handle the hot potato of being accepted as we are? We mumble, "Oh, come on! What are friends for!" If others don't discount us, we discount ourselves.

To dissipate the destructive force with which we have lived so long, we can change our perception. We can refuse to give it weight. I spoke of this before; it can be a kind of rationalization.

Another more ambitious way of encouraging only life-giving force is to stop evaluating. Look and describe. Stop judging. We can stop trying to manipulate and control others. We can stop being certain and begin to cooperate in a common search for answers. We can allow ourselves to be spontaneous, rather than working out of a strategy. We need to trust ourselves more. We can stop trying to be "brains on stilts," pretending we can deal with others without feeling. That's impossible. We may not own the feeling, but that doesn't dissolve it. Feelings are always present between people.

Am I dreaming? That we should ever treat each other so? Still, everything begins with a dream. The dream is often the father of the real.

MEETING

DREAMS

*D*reams are the children of imagination. They take on "flesh" from the stirrings of that part of us that never fully accepts reality. We experience those gentle yearnings that float just below our consciousness. They are revelations of our unknown self.

Nothing "new" has not first been dreamed. Dreams are the bearers of creativity. Lincoln dreamed of becoming president, facing defeat after defeat in the "real" world. Edison dreamed of the electric bulb on his lonely walks in Menlo Park. Henry Ford dreamed of a carriage without horses. Martin Luther King, Jr. dreamed of a country where all people were truly equal and free.

Some dreams come true. Others do not. Some are never forgotten. Others are lost. That loss does not mean that dreams are any less powerful. To pursue our dreams is to unleash a force within ourselves that must prevail. If we are defeated, others will pick up our dream, carrying it like an Olympic torch to its proper height.

> Are dreams so great that they can topple dams,
>   The dams of fear, suspicion and distrust?
>
> Only if the dreams are great
> And filled with hopes
> That all will call "impossible!"
>
> Our lives are hopeless without dreams
> That challenge us to bitter heights,
> That dare the very fears we all suppress.

To search is vain
Without the dream.
Only ruts and twigs and eaten trees,
That promise warmth and comfort,
Lie ready to be found.

But, dreamless, they are sterile and unkind,
Delivering neither promise nor reward.

A world at peace, the dream of Woodrow Wilson, is still a dream carried in the hearts of myriads of people. The pursuit of happiness, the dream of Jefferson and Adams, still strives for "flesh" in the fumbling efforts of our American government. The unity of all Christians is a dream waiting for birth in the souls of many Christians. A world without dreams is dead-ended. Life without hope is impossible. Dreams are the stuff out of which hope is made.

We make much of the need to act on our dreams, and so we should. But the opposite is also true: we would have nothing to act upon without our dreams.

Nightmares are also born of our imagination, but not of our hope. They are children of our fear, of our despair. They do not clothe our imagination in "flesh," for the worst rarely happens. I do not include nightmares in the wonderful world of dreams. Perhaps to do so would be too realistic for me, and I want to dream.

Jesus is sometimes called a dreamer and he probably is. He's so much like the Father. The world is the Father's dream enfleshed. The dream has not taken full form yet. Even Jesus was not sure of how it would all turn out. With its creation, the world, like most dreams, took on a life of its own. Probably the Father planned it that way. He likes a challenge.

Did Jesus inherit his love for a challenge from his Father? Probably. But, then, Mary was daring at times too. She stayed where men fled. She was at the foot of the cross. Peter was hiding, "not knowing the man."

Maybe to be God's child is to live with risk. Isn't faith risky? Blaise Pascal didn't think so, but he too was a dreamer. Dreamers seem not to cringe before risk. They are looking too far ahead to notice the risks they take, step by step. Their eye is on the goal, perhaps to be reached long after they have ceased to dream.

There are no dreams in heaven. They aren't needed. All has been fulfilled. I wonder if we dreamers will miss our favorite pastime? We'll probably be too fascinated by eternity to notice that dreams and challenges are no more. I hope so.

Here, in a world dreamed and created by God, fashioned in the image of Jesus, the Son and the dreamer, we need our dreams. Sometimes we lose sight of them and flounder in shallow reality. At such times we do not ask, "What makes life meaningful for me?" The question never occurs to us. We are taken up with "what is" or we don't care. Sometimes nothing matters. Then dreams keep their distance. They are not comfortable in such company.

Then, we are only half alive. We are busy, busy, busy. We are in demand. We are sought out and consulted. We are important. None of which means we are alive, if nothing matters. Life says "something matters," and that requires dreams. We need to dream of what can be. Denial and indifference belong in cemeteries. They make sense there.

We can kill each others' dreams. We can hurt enough to make dreaming stupid and silly. Cynicism rings out in hollow laughter at our dreams, and they scurry away blazed with blushes and frustration. They shall not appear again.

Unless we can talk with another. But that implies risk, and cynics don't trust easily. Trust would allow another to peek under the mask. In our hurtful disappointment we hug to ourselves the betrayed reality where a cold pretense of comfort is found. We don't want to talk because we might dream again, and be hurt again.

Why can't we talk?

Is love so fierce and fear so near
    That talktime has no place?
It is the urgency of the moment,
    The here, the now of hurt,
    That drowns tomorrow!

71

If mine is yours and yours is mine,
Why need we fear tomorrow?
  I have more questions than answers,
  More hopes than plans.
We cannot know "exactly" tomorrows,
  Because we are *today*.

But you do not understand:
  "I need the answers!"

Your need is a mirror,
  Only a mirror
  Of all you dreamed. It was so real!

"But real is where we are!"
So stops the talk,
And that's where we began.

When a dream has died, when talk is empty and useless, can we choose to dream again? The positive thinkers would say that we can do anything we want. Maybe they are right, or maybe they have dreamed themselves beyond our world. We can dream again, but it must be a different dream. Unlike people, dreams have no resurrection. Only what has become enfleshed can be resurrected. Recreating a dream that has died is as impossible as recreating a configuration of smoke that once hung in the air. Some things cannot bear tampering. Our merest touch changes them forever. Still, the dream is less important than the dreaming. Another will find our dream and match it to a world where the dream becomes a reality, for them. It is only important for us that we dream again and find our world that lets the new dream come true. All of us, not only cynics, must make peace with reality.

Dreams can be wishful thinking. They can hang endlessly in the air, whisked about by the years until time runs out. Real dreams thrust themselves onto reality, shaping it, framing it, stabilizing it for the dream's entry. At least they try to fashion reality for themselves, like the "form" of the Scholastic Philosophers who prepared it for its marriage with prime matter. They are not always successful, but that thrust is one criterion of a real dream. It makes us work to make it live. Wishful thinking is like a *voyeur*, daydreaming us into sleep. It is the friend whose kindness is cruel, refusing to point out that the emperor has no clothes.

Dreams change with the passage of years. Some disappear into reality, successfully coming alive and no longer needing the dream world. Some disappear from sheer exhaustion, unable to cope with the busy reality so hostile to their life. Some evolve into better and bigger dreams. Some are trimmed and clipped until they are the vestiges of their former selves. I suspect that all of these things are experienced by many of us.

I further suspect that those of us who think with our feelings and judge with our hearts are more aware of the ebb and flow of our dreams. The more logical, rational, and reasoned we are, the less we may be distracted by dreams. But all of that is only a guess, and one experience is no better than the other.

In a sense, dreams are like clouds. Some of us notice them faithfully, day by day if not hour by hour. Others of us notice only their absence or their rainy presence. And how life is treating us has a lot to do with it.

> Are clouds that fashion wishes
>   Like herrings in a school
> Indicative that dreams come true
>   If settled in a pool?
> Or are they fly-by-nights
>   That make no sense at all?
>
> When I was five I used to think
>   That clouds were meant for real
> But now that I am fifty-one
>   Clouds cannot really feel.
>
>   They aren't alive.
>   I feel deprived!
>
> Perhaps when I am older
>   I'll think that clouds are nifty!

> But that depends on what life is
> When I have turned to sixty.

The best time to dream is when we are in love. Love seems to have an affinity for dreams. Each alone can bring out the best in us and both together are unbeatable. We climb mountains, sail limitless seas, and look into eternity under the tutelage of love and the dream. Both are God's call to be ourselves, to be as complete and fulfilled as he intends us to be.

Love makes the impossible possible. It is the gatekeeper of our finest dreams, the physician removing scales that hide countless roads from us, the guide illuminating vistas long ignored. No wonder it is the soil rich with dreams long unsuspected.

Could Jesus have endured his crucifixion without love, without a dream? He never said. Each of us has to answer for ourselves. The dream yields what obedience cannot conceive. We need more lovers and dreamers and fewer compliers. But that's a dangerous path for organizations and institutions. It requires that we trust people. The institution never did see Jesus as trustworthy. It still doesn't. He's too ambiguous, a dreamer.

But does it matter? People are more important than institutions. Institutions are meant to serve people. Somewhere things went wrong. That's why compliance is so valued, love so suspect, and dreams so ignored. Many of us have come to believe that this is the way things should be. Any practice left long enough becomes the ideal. Only the dreamer questions it, and then is left ignored or patronized. But. . . we could dream this not to be so. . .

Can you hear the silence? An "ideal" has been questioned. Shh! Or do you hear "Tradition!" from the musical *Fiddler on the Roof?*

Dreams can be dangerous. The French Revolution was a dream, horribly executed. The American Revolution was a dream. The Communist movement is a dream. Dreams do not always follow absolutes or principles. They don't follow at all. They lead. That makes them dangerous.

Still, without dreams caves would still be our homes, hunting and gathering our pursuits, and matriarchy our culture. Cities, nations, governments would be unknown. Some of us might like that. I, for one, would like to have seen more matriarchy remain, but not at the price of a dreamless world. Even the dreamless like some of the results of dreams. The children of dreams are all about us; only their paternity is unknown. So, the parents, still among us, are passed by. If dreams can be dangerous, how much more the dreamer. Best we ignore them.

But we don't and we never will. There is a bottomless fountain in all of us that believes in infinity. Man and woman are immortal and limitless. God agrees. So, often enough we hear the dreamer, follow his tune and take another giant step toward the noosphere of Chardin. The dreams of "paper," "ink," "book," "printing press," and "computer" have transformed and will transform our world. Dreams have an irresistible attraction to us. They offer hope.

MEETING

FAILURE

*I*f ever I have doubted the "gentle touch" it is in failure. But failure is only temporary for dreamers. A new dream replaces the old. Hope springs eternal.

Failure can be only in the eyes of others, but that never stopped me from doubting my own perspective. We are contaminated by the views of others. Many years ago I left a vocation and career for which I had prepared over a decade. It was a victory decision, perhaps one of the few big, right decisions of my life. Other saw it differently, still see it differently, and that bothers a bit. It shouldn't, but none of us live in a vacuum. We Libras, particularly, find pain in seeing too many sides of the picture. We feelers find anxiety in our empathy with others.

Success for me in the eyes of others would have been failure in my own eyes. What appeared as failure to others was success for me. We manufacture pain for each other so that we don't have to feel pain ourselves. Perhaps so that we don't have to look too hard at our own choices. The other being right doesn't fit into our *weltanschauung,* our "philosophy of life." Everyone should live as "I" do. No surprises, please.

Failure in our own eyes is the worst because it is real. Others are not responsible for it, circumstances did not force it, nor evil people concoct it. We know when we have done it to ourselves. The sick feeling in the pit of our stomach tells us so. It is the dream smashed, the hope abandoned, the confusion in full blossom. An anchor has pulled loose; we have no orientation. Only the Irish write poems about it.

Original sin is not our failure but it acts as though it were.

We are born disoriented, we have no place to go. Our mind and will are fully intact but without a goal. We are made for fulfillment in God, but it takes a lifetime to get on course. Meanwhile, all of us are searchers. We search for meaning, for the significant other, for the words that will make sense of the experience. During all of which "Christian tradition" hints that we are "not all there," our "intellect has been darkened and our will weakened." We may suspect that we are idiots writing a philosophy of life! What has been "darkened and weakened" is our purpose. Our machinery works fine, but we don't know what it is for.

Real failures operate the same way. They take the form of divorces, alienated children, wrong life paths too long pursued and now unchangeable, vocations and careers wrongfully abandoned, and drugs allowed to "call the shots." Some of these may be sham failures, caused by circumstances or by others. I am writing about those we bring upon ourselves. In the grip of failure we have no purpose. Everything might be working but we aren't going anywhere. It's like starting from birth, from scratch. You would think that we would learn from original sin, but we don't. Some may even think that is the way life is meant to be! Lifetime disorientation tends to become an assumption, a given.

There is no way to convert failure; it is a diehard misery. We have tried every way we know how to make it a "bonus," but the pain remains. Failure is failure is failure. So, we may learn from it, grow from it, and be a better person for it. There are, however, too many other pleasurable ways to learn, to grow, and to become better instead of relishing our failures. How many of us have ever said, "Yippee! I failed today!"

How, then, do we meet failure? By acknowledging that it is a miserable experience and recognizing that we will probably do it again. Failure and life seem to go together. If we do not experience real failure, we are bound to experience sham failure. We trust when we shouldn't, are open when we should be closed, and choose to act when we should vegetate. Circumstances and others do us in, but a sham failure can be almost as painful as a real one.

Take Jesus. The crucifixion was a sham failure, but pain and death were no less than had they been real. People, institutions, and even friends conspired to effect it. The promise of resurrection did not make it "good," lessen the suffering, or make death more palatable. Family, confidants, and followers saw the crucifixion as nothing but failure. Only a few were to see its vindication in the resurrection and some Scripture scholars even dispute these few today. So, if Jesus didn't avoid failure. . . .

Sham failure pursues the idealist like the wolf pursues its prey. The idealist with lofty aspirations, dreams of change, and appetite for difference mightily tempts failure. Sometimes failure resists the temptation, and then we have the wonderful and the new that can be born of a dream. More often the temptation is too great and failure gives in. Failures are used to justify the thought that dreams are only for poets. The failures happen frequently enough to convince most of us that sticking our head above the crowd is not healthy. We remain in the flow, slightly bored, slightly dissatisfied, and slightly dead.

Fortunately, some of us continue to risk failure, knowing that only if we give up enfleshing our dreams will we not fail. Those who do nothing never fail. Or do they?

Peter, John, and the other apostles had real failures. Their infidelity was not brought on by circumstances or institutions, They chose to abandon the Christ. They risked doing something, following a leader whose future grew darker with every message he delivered. Before Jesus came around they were ordinary folk, eking out a living in whatever way they could, even by collecting taxes. They were family men lost in the crowd. Had they let Jesus go on his way they probably would never have failed. Or would theirs have been the greatest failure of all?

Some failures go unrecognized. There is the unseen failure of doing nothing out of fear, out of ambition, or out of indifference. I suspect many of us successful people live with this invisible companion, not even knowing that we do. The executive who has climbed to the top by silencing his/her ideals and principles, the bishop who has renounced his early disillusionment and its accompanying call to action, and the father who has modeled the pursuit of money for his children all live with failures that will not show themselves in this life. For them, that may be the worst thing about an afterlife: there is still time for revelation.

Other failures are only suspected. The wrangling and conflict that flows through too many marriages are indicators of suspected failures. They begin with distrust, a tingling recognition that the person with whom we spent our honeymoon no longer respects us. We suspect that we are living failures, but it is never said and, therefore, all the more credible. It is too disappointing, too shameful, to discuss. Anyway, it's hopeless. We cannot climb on our pedestal again, so it is assumed, so it is suspected. We are the cauldron within whom the ferment brews: a mixture of our poor self-image, our assumptions, and our distrust of the other. In this strange way many of us work very hard to prove ourselves failures. Suspicion can be the father of real failures. We could reject our suspicions and renounce our assumptions before real failure could happen. I think that works. Try it and watch the world change. We create the world around us, with all due respect to B.F. Skinner. Nurture and nature only touch the surface. We sculpt what we will.

We train ourselves in suspicion and distrust between the ages of three and four. My son, Patrick, is doing a fine job on himself right now. When, in his perception, his brother, Christopher, is receiving too much attention, Patrick acts on his suspicion and becomes most irritating. He screams out answers to questions, refuses to let his aunt or mommy sit in a particular chair, and continues exasperating behavior until he is sent to his room or spanked, or both! Now, that proves his suspicions, doesn't it? Mommy and daddy like Christopher better! They do nice things for Chris, but look what they do to me! Patrick has successfully proven his suspicion to be true. Now the ground is fertile for the creation of an assumption: "I am a failure. People only tolerate me." And off Patrick goes, fully prepared to prove he is a failure and disliked. Of course, it may not turn out that way. The sun may come out when he turns four. I hope so, but endings aren't always happy.

Some of us never age beyond three and a half. We pursue failure like Midas pursued gold, not satisfied until all we touch fails. Only then can we bask in the gloom of our own "truth."

What has always amazed me is our power to turn all of this around. There is a kind of mystical relationship between our expectations and the happenings around us. There is much more than is known to self-fulfilling prophecy. Perhaps it is the tip of Chardin's noosphere, the power of the mind over the universe.

It is not infallible. Even optimists fail. It does not lessen the need for caution and for planning. It is more like an environment within which we live, a current that flows through all that we do. As trite as it sounds, it is an attitude. It is couched in the cynic's, "Expect nothing and you won't be surprised." Many of us are comfortable with this dictum scratched above the entrance to our lives. But if that has proven true for us, so can its opposite, "Expect everything and you won't be surprised." Maybe that's the difference between success and failure. It's "all in the mind." And my tongue is not in my cheek.

Our expectations take the measure of our failure in other ways, less subtle and obscure. What is failure for one may be success for another. The successful businessman who wanted to be a physician can live with a brooding sense of failure. The maintenance man who becomes a manager may feel only success. We define our own failure. Sometimes others help, but we don't need to let them.

The resurrection of Jesus was not expected, perhaps not even by Jesus himself. In fact, it was not even needed to prove Jesus' success. Jesus knew he would be successful if he remained open to the father. Success for him was where that trust led. It happened to lead to the crucifixion, and for Jesus that was success. He had given all he could give. That was his aim in life and he achieved it. His expectations marked the difference between success and failure.

His churches soon forgot his expectations. They insisted you be Coptic, Roman, Greek, or Western to be Christian. Failure for them was non-conversion to a culture and race. Openness to the father was not enough. You had to think, act, and live as they did. We are still paying for that failure, unacknowledged and repeated too often. Jesus trusted, not knowing where his trust would lead. *We* thought we knew where we were going and trusted only ourselves. Smugness is a frequent companion of failure.

For me the greatest failure is to be untrue to myself, to lie to myself, to live dishonestly. But that is my choice, rooted in my own expectations. For you there may be other failures that are greater. Each of us must answer for himself or herself. The answer is important, for while we may weather many failures it is the greatest failure, as we see it, that will most certainly destroy us. That failure leaves us with nothing.

None of us can look in the mirror at a person without failure, for that would be to be without sin. Only one person in all of history could have done that. Still, there are different kinds of sins and different kinds of failure. What one survives another cannot. The failure we need most to fear is that which denies ourself, the one that would so change us that we would not recognize ourselves in any mirror anywhere.

MEETING
OURSELVES

*F*ew of us know ourselves. Most of us find nothing more interesting than a discussion about ourselves. Astrologers and fortune tellers have a very attentive audience. Salesmen exploit our ignorance of ourselves by building on needs we think we have and by giving us needs we never thought of. If we thought we truly knew ourselves we would have no fear of psychologists, psychiatrists, or professional feedback from human relations trainers. There is something fearful about finding out about ourselves and something irresistible about talking about what we think we know of ourselves. The search for real self-knowledge is a reluctant one.

A boss I once had loved to proclaim in his bombastic fashion, "Well, I'm never going to change!" He was insensitive, self-centered, cruel, short sighted, and irrational. His management style belonged in the 1920s. You get the picture. He had read all of the self-help books and listened to all of the self-development cassettes, attended many professional development workshops, and could spout the "in" words of self-knowledge with the best of Dale Carnegie's instructors. But what was in his brain never made it to his heart. That must have hurt with a pain never expressed except, I think, by, "I'm never going to change!" It hurts not to like yourself. He spent hours degrading others so that he would look good to himself. It didn't work.

That's a risk we take when we meet ourselves. We might not like what we meet. We'll probably try to handle the pain in any way we can, except to change. We see that as even more painful than living with what we have.

I keep meeting myself in my children, either by way of similarity or of contrast. They highlight for me long forgotten behavior, behavior that has so faded into my personal style that I no longer notice it. And, in some instances, I am tempted to change them before they make my mistakes. I think it will be easier to change them than to change myself. It won't be and it isn't. They will listen no better than I listened. For me not to try, however, would be to betray them.

We want to give our children the autonomy, the confidence, and the clarity of purpose we only partially achieved. Somehow or other we got the impression that we would work with "blank" little people born of our bodies. Perhaps the *tabula rasa* of the Scholastic Philosophers, the theory that children are born like a blank sheet of paper waiting to be written upon, influenced us, or me at least, more than we realized. We think we can mold anew what we have spent a lifetime creating.

It seems to me that we know our children better than we give ourselves credit for, provided we know ourselves. They are not carbon copies, but they are often striking facsimilies. In time, they may become even more striking contrasts, but few children start out that way. Imprinting is too strong where confusion surrounds helplessness.

I didn't always think that way. In my pre-parent days I used to wonder how I could love an unknown stranger growing from our bodies.

> How do you love without knowledge?
> How do you love a stranger?
>   With hope and fear and anticipation,
>   But without a proper solicitation?
>
> She's big, he's small,
> He's broad, she's tall,
> I guess all's possible with love
> And hopes and dreams fashioned above.
>
> 'Tis true, it seems
> We can love our dreams,
> Cottoned with candy
> And dripping with honey.

84

She's-he's fifteen inches
And eight pounds of right,
Ready to start on eternal flight!
Part of the family, part of God's Son,
Now ready to be a person,
A plus one.

We resolve to help our children become themselves, to become their own persons. We shall not make them like us. Yet, I suspect, their likeness to us is what makes them loveable to us. Too soon we find ourselves telling them what to do, what to think, and what to be. In spite of ourselves we teach conformity, perhaps at the price of our children's dreams. But we too once had dreams.

No matter what the weather in summer, fall or spring,
No matter that winter snows might still be lingering,
We'll love you in the autumn,
We'll love you in the fall,
In seasons good or bad, we'll be at your call!

No dreams can match your beauty,
No season match your calm,
No love can match your giving,
For you are giving all.

We accept! We accept!

We want you for yourself.
Don't be what others tell you to be.
Don't see what others tell you to see.

Do what you are.
See what you see.

Be proud of yourself.
Be proud that you be.

We parents seek immortality by creating people to our own

image and likeness, in spite of our dreams and resolves. Unless we are God, this is dangerous. We are working from incomplete blueprints. Only God knows himself perfectly. Only God has the right to create sons and daughters in his image and likeness. Only God can look at a son and see himself.

Meeting ourself is not a luxury. Our self-knowledge ripples like an invisible force through all that we do and all that we touch. Our self-styled wisdom is too often myopic tradition thoughtlessly accepted, our discipline stunts rather than channels, our compassion can have cruel consequences and our love can squeeze so hard that only shells of people are left. And all the time we think we are doing what is right.

Still, meeting ourselves does not always mean change, even if we don't like ourselves. Often it means acceptance. We need ask no more of ourselves than we ask of others: to accept us as we are. Strangely, that in itself can spark change and growth.

Feeling good about ourselves makes us want to feel better about ourselves. We are more ready to prune a fruitful tree to grow more fruit than we are to revitalize a dying tree. There is something attractive about making good better. Perhaps there is less chance of failure?

Jesus used this strategy. He wanted us to believe we are sons and daughters of God. Once we believed that, he knew there would be no stopping us. Life would be joyous, laughter would come easily, and suffering would have meaning. Jesus didn't stay with us long enough to show how self-acceptance would help us to become bigger and bigger through the years. He grew too fast to need to linger. Most of us take longer to catch up with him at thirty-three.

There is one kind of self-acceptance that stunts growth. It is the self-acceptance of the successful. We smile patronizingly at those who would tell us to change. We are successful. What we know about ourselves we like, and the rest doesn't matter. There's the rub. We look only at what has contributed to our success. We ignore those parts of ourselves that keep us from sleeping, keep others away, and keep hurting without need. I know. I was there once. Had I stayed there, had I not changed, I probably would continue to be "successful," but the cost to myself and to others would have been high. Too high, I think. Nothing is worth paying for with the loss of happiness, the loss of self-respect, and the loss of ideals. If you have paid these three coins there is little left to give to yourself, to others, or to God. There are too many unhappy "successes" already.

Real success comes from meeting ourselves and accepting the consequences, much like staying with a friend through thick and thin. To do otherwise is to use ourselves, to use our friend for unworthy spoils. We cannot escape ourselves unless we want to spend all of our lives in a masquerade parade. Mardi Gras and Jumbalaya are fun only as long as we know the faces are masks that can be taken off. Only gods are happy as gods, devils as devils, and monsters as monsters. They are to enjoy, not imitate.

When we meet ourselves we need to meet all of ourselves, not only those sides of self we think are important. Often the unimportant sides cause us and others the greater misery. We are brilliant but insensitive, witty but cynical, caring but self-centered. So, we discount insensitivity, cyncicism, and self-centeredness. We may even baptize them to be autonomy, realism, and self-caring for the service of others. But they are still insensitivity, cynicism, and self-centeredness. The baptism never takes, except to our blind eyes. For self-acceptance to work, we need to accept all of ourselves for what we are. When we start rationalizing we know we want to hide something. When we start discounting, we know we want to avoid changing. We know we have died without burial when we say, "Why should I change? Look how successful I am as is."

We meet ourselves in our friends. Have you ever noticed how alike friends often are? Beautiful women make friends with beautiful women. If we are young our friends are often young. Like attracts like. Flower lovers travel with flower lovers. Fanciers of automobiles seek out the company of fanciers of automobiles. Our tastes pull us together. Still, that is rather superficial. Perhaps we are attracted to those who we like to think are mirrors of ourselves. But these are often acquaintances, not friends.

An old sage once said that we are fortunate to have one or two real friends during a lifetime. If we look to our acquaintances to learn about ourselves we are likely to find what we want to find. In fact, of course, we may find only a mirage, wishful thinking about what we like to think we are. Real friends don't allow that. Love lets them share their perceptions without contamination. The problem is that we don't listen, and the moment is lost.

"To see ourselves as others see us," as Robert Burns would want, is a confusion we rarely enjoy. We feel that both feet are off the ground at the same time and that doesn't leave much in our control. It's scary. But the prize is worth the price. There is the moment of "Aha!" that explains so much about our personal experiences. It is a moment of glowing intuition akin to a mystical experience that can shape the rest of our life. We shall not forget the friend who led us into the light that all except ourselves have always seen.

For some of us Jesus is the friend who lifts the curtain. In contemplation we find a picture of ourselves where all the pieces fit. We can be fooled, of course. We mistake our own voice for that of the Lord, paint our picture with our own colors rather than let Jesus do the painting. No wonder we like what we see. We are too busy getting the composition just right to hear what the Lord has to say. Like Narcissus we have fallen in love with ourselves and little energy is left for honest communication. We may even revel, as did some saints, in being the worst of sinners. Then we can take comfort in being little boys and girls whom our parents love in spite of our naughtiness. Even contemplation can screw us up.

In fact, I think that the gift of self-knowledge from the Lord is rare. Perhaps some of the saints received it, but if we are to believe the doleful pictures of self painted by such as Augustine and Theresa, the Little Flower, many of the saints were deceived. Neurosis, not prayer, was the canvas upon which they painted.

All of which does not mean we shouldn't pray. It does mean that we should not *only* pray. Self-knowledge grows in a climate of personal integrity and honesty. It matures when we are able to hear what is happening in our lives. We hear and evaluate messages that come from friends and experience.

I have a friend whose prayer at the end of each day takes the form of a reflective evaluation of the day's events, looking at them in the full detail of recent memory and evaluating them in the light of his philosophy of life. He finds what fits into what he says hc is and resolves to repeat that kind of behavior. What does not fit he questions. Is it a part of himself he has not met before? Does he want to change that? Does he want to accept it? Is it a sign of growth or decay? He learns a lot about himself that way. It may be a way to go.

Central to meeting ourselves is meeting our sexuality. Freud may not be entirely accurate, but few of us would say that sexuality is not a master key to understanding ourselves, if we are honest. Sexuality has colored our upbringing, our education, our relationships, our minds, and our choices. There is no meeting ourselves without meeting our sexuality.

MEETING
SEXUALITY

When I was six sex was boring. At twelve it was confusing and at sixteen it became a mysterious force I had to handle. In time it became a reflection of God in whom persons become one in love. I learned how to theologize it, how to reason about it. I learned, by forty, that my sexuality affected all that I am, my thinking, my choosing, and my living. Sexuality was not genital, it is total. I think that's what we mean when we speak of sexuality rather than sex.

For thousands of years God has tried to tell us about sex and sexuality. First, he suggests, comes sensuality, the experience of the five senses when they "do their thing." The experience of a floating sunset in the Caribbean, the relief of a cool breeze on a scorching summer day, the chirping of robins and blue jays in our backyard, and the taste of good food are some of our sensual delights. Early on, God said "You may eat indeed of all the trees in the garden" (Genesis 2:16b).

Sexuality is a pervading set of inclinations, attitudes, and tastes that are part of sexuality, the part that distinguishes male and female characteristics, psychological and physical. God saw that sexuality needed relationship, and so he created woman (Genesis 2:23). This chapter is about sexuality. Sexuality is not black or white. Men possess some aspects of female sexuality, and women possess some aspects of male sexuality. We shall reflect on this very shortly.

Sex is the label we give to distinguish male from female according to sexual organs. It is physical, perhaps the most obvious physical expression of sexuality. Sex problems are usually medical problems. Problems of sexuality involve the total person.

Thomas á Kempis wrote that he would rather feel compunction than know its definition. After all of my thinking and reasoning about sexuality and sex I feel akin to á Kempis. Sexuality is best understood emotionally.

The celebration of marriage says more about the meaning of sexuality than all of the learned tomes written from the time of Aquinas to the time of Fromm. Like God, sexuality seems to defy description. It is physical, it is spiritual, it is singular, it is common, it is sacred, it is human. It is as complex as the human condition, a mixture of the sublime and the dust from which we come.

Of one thing I am almost sure: Like God, sexuality is necessary. Necessary not in the sense of Wilhelm Reich, who could conceive of no personal growth without its experience, but in the sense of its power. Would God have made it so powerful if it were not necessary? Perhaps he feared that we would never communicate well enough, never get close enough to each other, were we not "forced" to do so. Sexuality is the strongest unifying force in the world.

Both church and state have recognized this from the earliest of times. If we control the sexuality of others, we control them totally. Church and state do so under the guise of establishing order and structure for society, perhaps not aware themselves of their real motivations. We value order and structure that nurtures a civilized society, laws that identify marital rights and obligations and that protect our sensibilities from the degradations to which sexuality can drag us, but it is good to recognize the price we pay for such order and decency.

Some philosophers say that nothing has meaning until we give it meaning, but it seems to me that sexuality doesn't need us to label it. It unifies, at least initially, whether we like it or not. It may become deeply divisive, bringing nations to war and churches to fragments, but isn't that because nations and churches use it for control? It seems that way sometimes.

Regardless of what nations and churches do, however, I have to learn to live in peace with my sexuality. If anyone is to control it, or to use it, that person is me. The problem is that it is so close to me, and I often find that the closer I am to something, the more difficult it is to understand. I could use a little myopia on occasion.

The first thing I know about my sexuality is that it is persistent. I don't mean that it is always demanding, requiring genital expression. Psychologists suggest that our sexual organ is our brain. Successful therapy gives credence to their contention. And our thinking is persistent, even when we sleep. So, my sexuality is on the job 24 hours a day, seven days a week! I think, reason, decide, like, dislike, and react according to my sexuality. No wonder it can cause so much trouble.

My sexuality is a part of all of my relationships. How it expresses itself often influences the quality and depth of the relationship. I am attracted to my wife by my sexuality, attracted to my friend Jim by our common values and tastes, and attracted to my God by my need for dependence and fulfillment. My need for a mate, for friends, and for God are all colored by my sexuality. There is a genital need and a complementary need. I love because I need to give and to receive as a man, and as a woman. Because I am a man I relate to others differently than a woman. That's a given for most of us.

Still, my male sexuality may not be the same as my brother's male sexuality. In me I find the capacity to care for my infant with joy, to write verse to say what cannot be said in prose, and to do string art and macrame. My brother has no such inclinations. His male sexuality is of a different mix than mine. But it is my own sexuality with which I must be comfortable.

We are not comfortable when we pretend. I am not comfortable when I play "John Wayne," but I hope John Wayne was. If we need to accept ourselves we need to accept our sexuality most of all. We are sexual creatures in all that we do, each in a uniquely different way. We are our sexuality. The celibate and the virgin are sexual creatures who do not express their sexuality in a genital way. Sexuality is not "genitality." That would be too limiting.

For other animals sexuality and genitality are the same. They are sexual only in the mating season. We are sexual all the time. Perhaps that is why we have no mating season.

My sexuality was not fully developed at birth. It was built layer upon layer through the years. It started, of course, with my male genitals. That made Mom and Pop decide to raise me in a particular way, my sister to treat me as a brother, my first playmates to deal with me as a boy, and my first teachers to class me as a male. Along the way I was lucky enough to have a girl-friend who may have been responsible for sharing something of the female with me, and I'm sure my mother did much of the same.

Few of us are pure males or pure females. Our sexuality is a mixture of characteristics we somewhat arbitrarily label male or female. It seems to me that we need that mix because communication requires that there be something of me in you and of you in me. We need to have a mix. Without it we probably would be pretty lonely. Physical sex deprived of any tangential relationships is lonely business. Ask any prostitute.

Ask Mary Magdalen. Her relationship to Jesus was not one of physical sex, yet it was more powerful than any of the relationships to which she thought she was doomed. It transformed her. Why? Because Jesus is God? Maybe. I like to think that she found something of herself in Jesus and of Jesus in herself so that real communication took place. She could understand and be understood, much like we understand and feel understood when we meet a fellow spirit. Not only opposites attract.

Jesus treated physical sex almost casually. Adultery was not on his mind when he saved the woman caught in that sin from stoning. He saw the guilt of humankind who are too ready to judge, unmindful of their own condition. He saw hypocrisy and the brutal use of law to bolster our own sense of self-righteousness. He did not condone adultery but neither did he ever rail against it as he railed against the hypocrisy of the Pharisees.

When asked about marriage and celibacy Jesus responded with only a sentence: "It is not everyone who can accept what I say, but only those to whom it is granted" (Matthew 19:11). When asked about divorce his answer was a quote from the Old Testament and three sentences to uphold the indissolubility of marriage (Matthew 19:4-9). But his talk on the Beatitudes and at the Last Supper on love were lengthy and complete. Love of others, justice to all—the deeper and more demanding aspects of our sexuality were far more important to Jesus than how to use our sexual organs. Christianity waited for Paul before it became disturbed about that part of our sexuality, and it seems like it may never get over that obsession and return to the priorities of Jesus. But there is always hope.

Christianity consecrates the use of our body by revealing to us the presence of the Spirit within each of us. We are temples of God, just as Jesus spoke of his own body. So physical sex is not unimportant. The sharing of ourselves leaves us nothing more to give, at least physically. That is why it is the ultimate expression of human love most of us can achieve. We have endowed intercourse with that meaning, and it is in keeping with the spirit of the Jesus who gives us his body.

For the Christian, sharing *only* physical sex is hypocrisy. We lie about our relationship, about who we are, and about what we mean. We destroy ourselves and others because physical sexuality is the way we express our commitment. If sexuality is ourself, at the core of our personality and identity, physical sex is its ultimate expression. I think it takes some time to understand that, just as it takes time to become Christian.

Even those of us whom God "touches gently" find that meeting our sexuality is unsettling, at least in puberty. Some of us spend a lifetime sorting it all out, and that's OK as long as we continue to sort it out. Like so many other things in life, we lose only if we give up the search.

Sexuality is part of our sensuality. Its discovery in our young years is bewildering and disturbing. I am speaking not of the sensual pleasure we take in walking in the rain, swimming, or other physical activity (although these pleasures, too, are part of our sexuality), but of the sexual stirrings that are part of human growth and living. Sometimes our sexuality is so disturbing that it becomes an obstacle to our search for maturity and personal integration. I have suspected that this is particularly true of those raised in a religion that labels sex "dirty" before we even know what it is. But I may be talking only from my own experience. If we feel guilty about our sensuality, we feel guilty about our sexuality and, therefore, about ourselves.

We need to dismantle the Scholastic notion of natural law which makes it so easy to define right and wrong with arrogant certitude. In our rush to keep our children pure we have stunted the personal growth of many and intensified the struggle for the rest. We need to teach sexuality as a drive for unity among all peoples, the deep personhood that gives all of us value, and the anchor we need to control our own lives. We need to feel good about ourselves, so that we can grow and allow others to grow. Then we may not have to worry so much about sin. Certainly making ourselves and others feel guilty has not worked.

MEETING
BELIEF

*B*elief starts easy. We believe in God because "grown-ups" say he is so. That's easy, like believing in Santa Claus or the Easter Bunny. We want to believe. We love the world of pretend.

My own path to belief was the Roman Catholic tradition, so you will find this coloring in my reflections. While your starting point might be different, I think that pilgrims all have a common experience, at least fundamentally. This is a brief description of the salient points of my own journey until the present. I share it because it might apply to other journeys to faith.

As I grew up I found believing to be fun. It made me part of the important world of grown-ups. They seemed to think that religion was important, so I thought it was important. Following rules was mostly fun, and it made me feel superior to those who had no rules to follow. I was important enough to be expected to obey. Others could take the "easy" way. In my religion people knew who they were and had their place, and were all loved by God, of course.

Only gradually did I begin to suspect that following rules did not a believer make. Then believing was not so easy. The world became fuzzier, people lost their places and gray areas seemed to appear out of nowhere. No, I shouldn't say nowhere. Philosophers, theologians, and writers created the gray areas. Was Mary a virgin? If so, so what? Did Jesus really rise from the dead? What happened when we prayed? Did God really hear us? Answer us? Was bread and wine really necessary for the Eucharist, or could we use cake and cookies? Was the pope infallible? Then why so many mistakes? Were Luther and Henry VIII right? How about Galileo? Was the church of Jesus still with us, one, holy, catholic, and apostolic? It didn't seem to be one...or holy...or.... Theologians who in my youth had given tortured explanations of vested claims now questioned the unquestionable. Things were gray indeed.

Belief is always gray. Were it clearly black or white only the irrational would be unbelievers. We believe the stranger who gives us directions, the doctor who gives us medicine, the taxi driver who promises to take us where we want to go. We only believe when we do not know. No wonder hope goes with faith: without trust there is no belief. Only the blind can believe, for the blind see gray.

Jesus, John, and Augustine seemed to have the right idea: "Love and do what you want." Love is blind, a commitment in gray. We believe in another, trusting with vulnerability and committing ourselves without reserve. There are no rules for the lover. The lover doesn't need them. Jesus gave rules only when asked for them, I suppose with the hope that the questioners would someday grow up.

Still there is a part of me that whispers, "People need rules. You can't trust love." Maybe that's the little boy in me who wants to feel superior and comfortable, secure in the knowledge he is good because he follows the rules. Or maybe it's the philosopher in me that requires rules for good government. I keep hearing, "Rules make us free," but that sounds too much like the tortured explanation of yesterday.

The believer in me has no trouble with believing without rules. I know rules protect and nurture civilization, that they provide boundaries and guarantee rights, and that anarchy is not desirable. All of that comes from my mind. And that is why it does not apply to belief.

Belief is too personal to be confined to the brain. It is personal in the sense that it embraces my whole person. Belief is no more intellectual than love. It is a choice about all that I am and want to be, giving an orientation and direction that makes sense of life. Belief gives meaning, but I suspect that belief is not in the service of meaning. We don't believe so that life will make sense. Life makes sense because we believe.

Education seems to slice off pieces of belief. Scripture scholars teach us that the story of creation is not to be taken literally. Church historians tell us that celibacy was not the Christian ideal until many centuries after Christ left us and that popular devotions, religious holidays, and Christmas, were originally adaptations to pagan customs created to quiet the multitudes. Between the lines we even learn to suspect that the commandments came from the legal mind of Moses and not from God's love.

We can shut our ears and eyes to such "ravings," and many of us do. Ignorance can be very peaceful. It offers few challenges. Then I give in to the little boy (or girl) in me. I can continue to believe that God *owes* me if I believe his word.

We can swallow such "ravings" whole and with a flip of the "if" switch can cease to believe. "If Mary is not a virgin, *then* none of this stuff is true." That's an easy route, especially for those of us who saw little point in believing in the first place. It's also an easy route for the lazy. It is easier to construct a flippant syllogism than to continue the search for the real Jesus.

Persistent belief suspects that our theologians and historians are not raving when they do their job of reflecting on God's word. Those of us who are so stubborn begin to suspect that even the theologians and historians are chipping away at only the tip of the iceberg. There seems to be a massive construct of traditions and doctrines that began building almost before Jesus got back to his Father. The construct was made with good intentions by strong believers. It was made to teach the ignorant "children" with whom they wanted to share Jesus. But children would not understand how believers knew that Jesus is God unless...he was born of a virgin...worked miracles...and...rose from the dead. The believers wanted to tell us that Jesus was special, that he is truly God, that he always was, and always will be. But they didn't trust us to believe without describing the unbelievable life of Jesus.

It seems that the construct doesn't matter that much if we understand belief to be belief in a person, not a belief of a number of incredible facts and instances. Looking beneath the construct we discover that much of the construct is an effort at communication, a language that tells us about the person in whom we believe by using sign and symbol. The story of creation and the prologue of John tell us to look at the world around us if we want to know what Jesus is like: it was created in his image as he is the image of the Father. The construct of creation explains to us why the search for God is so long, obscure, and uncertain: because we have clouded the mirror of creation with our greed, our anger, and our brutality. That's the stuff out of which belief is made. We listen to the word, we listen to the community of believers, and we begin to glimpse a darkening of the outline of a person called Jesus.

Traditionally faith has been a "leap." It is not supported by doctrine or morals. They are significant only to better understand the person in whom we have chosen to believe. The person comes first, perhaps not logically, since we need to know the gospel story to first hear of Jesus. But mystically, once we have heard the word, then all the things about Jesus take second place to Jesus himself. Were this the message of the churches we would not have so many of them. Whether Jesus multiplied the loaves and fishes or motivated the crowds to share with each other is not a salvific question. The message is that Jesus is sensitive to our needs and his followers need to be sensitive to the needs of others. We always have to ask what the word tells us about the person of Jesus. Then our faith is saving and the "facts" have some meaning.

There are, of course, boundaries and limits to the interpretations we give to the facts of the word that necessarily are divisive. If we choose to interpret the facts to mean that Jesus is an ordinary person, an early version of Pope John XXIII or of Martin Luther King, Jr., our belief is quite different than if we were to see Jesus as divine, the son of God and one with the Father. Then we have to ask ourselves whether our belief in Jesus is faith or a profound belief and trust that we might have in any outstanding human. And then, we have to ask whether belief in a human is enough for us.

Our belief is colored by the company we keep. Early in life we find ourselves in a family and a community. We are impressed with values, attitudes, ideas, messages, and beliefs our community lives and breathes. We don't have to accept them, and some of us do not. Most of us do. For a short or long time we act on the values, beliefs, and attitudes of our community. We may or may not mature into accepting or rejecting those values, beliefs, and attitudes as our own. That is important for maturity.

Equally important is the tradition of our community. The Christian community holds within its memory the meaning of the facts that offer to us the opportunity to believe. My community interprets the facts of the life of Jesus to mean that Jesus is the Son of God. Your community might interpret those same facts to mean that Jesus was a great man or even a prophet. There is a difference, but not one to be resolved with bitterness and war. The Crusades assured the loss of that which they were meant to achieve.

Differences in belief about who Jesus is (or was) are important. I would not belittle them. Whatever our belief or non-belief in Jesus, however, I cannot conceive fighting over it. It would seem to be the last thing a savior of humankind would want. It seems much more important that our belief give meaning to our lives and to our deaths.

Belief cannot be dissolved by conflict, except at the personal level. History has illustrated that. At the personal level, however, disappointments, estrangement, and disillusionment have led believers into bitterness and rejection. "How could God, if there is a God, do this, allow this. . . ?" Our child dies, our spouse leaves us, we get cancer. Should we expect more of ourselves than bitterness and rejection? Perhaps. But bitterness and rejection are understandable. Jesus came close when he lamented, "My God, my God, why have you deserted me?" (Mark 15:34b) The tragedy is to allow our bitterness to endure. If Jesus showed us anything in the facts of his life, it is that he is loving. He may not think or act as we do, but he is Love. There is the linchpin of belief.

I used to worry about the Arab, the Jew, and the unbeliever. Then I met some. I don't worry as much any more. As much, if not more so, many have wrestled with the meaning of life and have come up with answers satisfying to themselves. And that is what it is all about. We need to have sense and meaning for ourselves. It is not a matter of good, better, best. It is a matter of orientation, direction, and significance. Then we have peace, and that is what Jesus left us. The "fire" he came to cast is the conflict we experience as we wrestle ourselves into a maturity where significance is important.

I'm with Carl Rogers and Teilhard de Chardin. Each of us, and the world around us, is driven to wholeness. God is found in many forms, perhaps even in the wholeness of the agnostic and atheist for whom this world is its own justification and significance. Life is its own reason for being. That can make sense and God is found in significance. Viktor Frankl was right on the mark: "I never tire of saying that the only really transitory aspects of life are the potentialities; but the moment they are actualized, they are rendered realities; they are saved and delivered into the past wherein they are rescued and preserved from transitoriness. For, in the past, nothing is irrevocably lost but everything is ir- revocably stored. Thus, the transitoriness of our existence in no way makes it meaningless."[1]

Frankl's point is that our choices dictate the shape of the world we live in. There may be hundreds of choices we could make, but none count except those that we do make. What we choose to do turns into reality and becomes part of our personal history. Only mere possibilities, those things not chosen, are lost and passing. But because what we choose to do is so permanent we need to appreciate the grave responsibility we have for the choices we make.

I suggest that each of us is responsible for finding meaning in life and that we do that with the choices we make. Those choices build a history and a reality that is always with us. What might have been is the only transitory aspect of life.

It makes no difference whether our choice is to live by a pro- ven principle of science or by an assumption. The product of our choice forever becomes part of reality. It is an assumption that mankind has a drive toward wholeness and meaning, so, in a sense, it is a belief. Like religious faith, it is a "leap." It seems to be part of the human condition to rest our lives on unfounded assumptions. We seem compelled to "leap" to significance if we want to make sense of life. For some, proven scientific principles may be enough to give life meaning. For others, meaning may not be important. For us believers, accepting assumptions seems inescapable.

The eighteenth-century philosopher, George Berkeley, tried to do away with belief by proposing that only God and ideas truly existed; all physical things existed only because our mind sug-

---

[1]*Man's Search for Meaning* (New York, N.Y.: Pocket Books, 1971), 190-191.

gested them. There had to be a God to give order to all that we perceived. Only irrational people could deny God. Berkeley's adversaries used to enjoy saying "Bishop Berkeley whispered darkly, 'If I don't see you, you don't be you!' " Perhaps I sound a bit like the bishop when I say that we need to build our lives on unfounded assumptions. I agree with the bishop only in the need to find significance in life without proof. We need to believe in God, in Jesus, in humankind or in ourselves, and belief with proof is not belief.

Belief is childlike. A child trusts his or her parents. There are no questions of their origin, their color, their religion, or their beliefs. Parents are there to love and to be loved. They are warm and caring, concerned and demanding. But children don't expect parents to prove themselves until later. Parents are a "given."

For the Christian believer God is a "given." There are other ways to find meaning in life, other "leaps" that can be made, but for here and now belief in God and in Jesus makes sense. With maturity and reflection, of course, it will be discovered that any "leap" leads to a "given." We cannot elude trust if we are to find meaning.

Belief is like a love affair that turns out well. We are attracted to another, progressing in our commitment until trust leads us to intimacy and complete vulnerability. Risk is always present. We cannot know how our vulnerability will be handled. We could be exploited or rejected. We could be appreciated and find the other vulnerable in return. When all goes well in love and belief, new life is born, goals are pursued, and every sunrise has a meaning.

I don't think we can believe without love. Belief in another requires a trust that is not likely without a sense of loving and of being loved. Lives are more visibly destroyed by disappointed love than by disappointed belief, but the destruction is no less complete. Judas was disappointed in himself, in his betrayal of love and belief. Love and belief were so intermingled they were one. So they are for us. Both require a choice, both require trust, and both require commitment. They are like the seamless robe of Jesus.

Unlike parents, belief and love ought never to have to prove themselves. They may be superficial, and it seems possible to live a life with surface belief and surface love. It seems possible to grow in every way except in belief, trust and love. We remain committed to a believing community, practice what is expected, and behave as anticipated. Perhaps that is enough. There is no need for proof.

I have found the need for more. Like so many others, I have questioned the believing community until I could make its convictions my own. Things were lost along the way, wrong roads taken and retraced, and the questions still come. I suspect this is not an uncommon experience today. We want to take a new look at the construct surrounding Jesus, to examine new meanings in the language of sign and symbol and to hear the thoughts of like spirits who are searching for the real Jesus. The search may be unnecessary and fruitless. The effort may be wasted. Still, it is a search and an effort that makes life meaningful. We search not for proof but for potentialities.

MEETING
THE FUTURE

Part of my belief is that there is a future for each of us. Because I'm an optimist (in my better moments), I think that future is a good one: universal nuclear war will not happen, nuclear power will reduce the cost of our utilities, and we shall have too many prisons without inmates. Our hospitals, like our schools today, and our prisons will be turned into educational resource and cultural centers. Cancer will be conquered. The television industry will regularly produce classics to rival Shakespeare and Verdi. Communism and capitalism will find a *via media*.

If you're becoming nauseous, I'll admit I'm not too certain about television producing classics. Perhaps they'll only discover themes other than boy-girl, wealth-power and cops-robbers.

I don't think you can be a card-carrying Christian without being an optimist. I can't imagine the *parousia,* the coming of Christ, coming on the heels of nuclear devastation, and I believe in the *parousia.*

We don't want to live in the future. The present is all that we truly have, but I have spoken about that before. Most of us cannot help but anticipate the future, some of us planning for years ahead while others of us are looking only to tomorrow. Sociologists tell us that the higher our income the further ahead we look; we are willing to delay today's pleasures so as to experience greater pleasures tomorrow. The poor often do not see beyond supper tonight. Greater resources, I suppose, allow us greater dreams. It is hard to plan for our child's education on an empty stomach. In one way or another, however, most of us anticipate a future.

I have not read any of Norman Vincent Peale's books but my experience has led me to believe in what I understand he means by the "power of positive thinking." The times I am confident about the future almost always create a successful future. If I allow myself to think a task is difficult, the task is difficult. When I convince myself I can do a job with ease, I do it easily. Try it yourself the next time you have to wrap yourself around a baby seat to secure your child with a safety belt or the next time you have to open a bottle of champagne.

There seems to be a mystical connection between our expectations and outcomes. Perhaps positive expectations improve our coordinations. I really don't know the reasons. It has been "proven" time after time in the field of teaching. Over the past few years experiment after experiment has shown that a teacher's expectations influence the performance of students. High teacher expectations produce superior student performance; low teacher expectations produce low student performance. We guess that our expectations are telegraphed to our students by our behavior, tone of voice, facial expressions, etc. But we really don't know the connection between expectations and performance. That's why I call the connection "mystical." If all teachers believed it and practiced it, little else would be needed to improve our educational system.

When we truly believe we can shape our future, as well as the future of others by our expectations we can come to feel terribly responsible. It is scary, but we don't want to become scrupulous. There are forces beyond our control I think!

Jesus expected great things of his mission, but they would come only after crucifixion and death. Positive expectations cannot assure us there will not be failures and difficulties. Positive expectations only promise ultimate success.

> When things have turned to earth and ash,
>   Events have had their way,
> Is that the time to say "enough,"
> Is that the time to pray?
>
> If life is meant to be hereafter
>   Perhaps that is the way.

But if *this* life is worth its salt
   Then we defend the day.

We plan, we plot, we think anew,
   Tomorrow's ever new.
Our life is not an obstacle,
   Its color is not blue.

The challenge leads to victory,
   The problem's only outcome.
If that's the way it seems to you
   You'll live *this* life
   And then some!

We cannot foretell the future, but we are responsible for it. The future is built out of our past and our present. Outside forces, hostile or friendly, touch us, chipping here and cutting there. The unexpected rises from ground we have ignored with our eyes on the stars. Surprises come at inopportune moments, but they would not be surprises if they did not. Ultimately, however, our expectations shape the future.

How do we shape our expectations? Is it O.K. to be unrealistic? Must we have plans and blueprints? Is dreaming enough?

Our expectations are shaped by our philosophy of life. My philosophy is that life is to be enjoyed, it is to be fun, so it seems quite reasonanble to me that our expectations should be a touch unrealistic. We don't want to set ourselves up for disappointment, but if our hopes are not a bit unrealistic they are probably pretty dull. We Christians entertain pictures of heaven that are unrealistic. Eternal happiness? Every need fulfilled? Time no more? Utopia beyond Thomas More? Doesn't that seem a bit unrealistic? But we expect just that, and we'll probably get it! That's the fun part of believing. To expect a heaven where we have only fame and fortune is drab in comparison.

Some people need plans and blueprints to structure their expectations, but it seems to me that most of us can't be bothered. We kind of fumble along. Oh, if we all planned, our life would probably be more successful, our businesses more profitable, and our family life more fulfilling. I suppose we don't plan because deep inside we think it is a waste of time. Plans have to be changed. Of course, plans are meant to be changed. We make plans to know where we are as we trudge or run the course of life. We change them to keep our direction and to measure our progress. But. . . that description never convinced us to plan. After all, we say, if we have to change them why make them?

I suspect, however, that we are fooling ourselves. As soon as we have expectations a subtle planning drifts into our lives. If our expectations are not pie-in-the-sky, but still a bit unrealistic, we begin to behave and act in ways to make them real. I think this happens unconsciously to all of us who refuse to "plan." We do so in spite of ourselves. In this sense, dreaming is enough. Real dreams come equipped with real plans. They are not available in the stripped down model.

If Jesus had a plan for his mission it is not obvious. He seemed to pick up his employees from the guys down the block, talk to anyone who happened to be around, and perform miracles at whim. Even the Last Supper appeared to be a last minute thought. He seems to have planned his last trip to Jerusalem, and that ended in crucifixion. So much for planning, we say. Of course, there is the resurrection, but we're not sure whether that was in the plan of Jesus or only in the plan of the Father.

We have plenty of ministers, priests, bishops, etc. who can tell us exactly the plan of Jesus. He planned to establish a church, to create sacraments, and to organize a hierarchy of authority with power to make choices for him. Our theologians and historians sometimes support such a plan. Scripture scholars tell us that the gospel writers even put words in Jesus' mouth to make sure we all understood this plan.

No doubt hindsight is better than foresight for discerning a plan. Once something has happened it is easy to see how it was planned. Dreams do come with plans, conscious or unconscious, and Jesus was a dreamer. He probably did have a plan but, like the plans of most of us, it was all in his head. It was more intuitive than detailed, more a sense of direction than a blueprint, more an attitude than a series of steps to be taken. Come the crucifixion he wanted to change the plan, but it was too late.

We plan the fulfillment of our expectations in our attitudes. Confidence in our expectations is a plan; our intuitive choice with an eye on our expectations is a plan; persistence in our expectations is a plan. Our plan takes the form of putting one foot in front of the other day by day as we pursue our dream.

Rarely can any of us achieve our future without help. Even Jesus sought the help of Peter, James, John, Mary, Joseph, and others. Expectations colored with greed, and those that are self-serving need others to be stepping stones "to the top." Such expectations understand "help" to mean "use:" people "help" us when they let us exploit them. Healthy expectations don't expect this kind of help because they don't look to a future built on the bruised bodies and souls of others. Healthy expectations need others to join with them in the pursuit of a future in which all involved can find satisfaction. The joining enhances the confidence, enjoyment, and persistence of the pursuit.

Are lives so fragile that they crash on every reef in storm?
Are hopes so lucid that all can plumb their depths?
Do we so live that life is simple, every moment scorned?
Or is there greater meaning?

Today foretells tomorrow,
This moment is forever,
This moment is today!

We love, we laugh, we dream—
Together now
We shall create the future,
You and I, together now!

As ugly and undesirable as fascism is as a form of government, its symbol, a number of reeds or rods bound together with a leather thong, is worth some reflection. Each reed alone can be easily broken, but bound together they have formidable strength. Each of us can be broken as we try to forge our future alone, but with the help of others we gather new strength to do what we know we have to do.

The gentle touch of the Lord is felt in the caress of our baby, of our friend and of our loved ones. Often it is only a look or an expression, but it strengthens us to move ahead, to persist, and to persevere until our expectations become a happening that used to be the future. Peter experienced the gentle touch in the look of Jesus after Peter had denied him. Augustine experienced it in the faith Monica placed in him, and Jung experienced it in Freud, at least for a time.

What do we do when we achieve our future? What do we do with success? Little has been said or written about meeting success. Perhaps the successful need no insights or reflection, or so we assume. But success can be destructive. It seems that we need to strive, to struggle toward a goal. When there are no goals we stagnate and even die. How often death follows retirement.

So, what do we do after our expectations have been fulfilled? We had better prepare to meet a new future. It is the key to life. And, after all, we never truly meet our future until we enter the new life of eternity. Then we shall see what we have felt all of our lives: the gentle touch.

I expect a future in which there will be:
—no anger behind steering wheels
—respect for you and me just because we are you and me
—time to be together
—work worthy of our talents
—nations that behave like reasonable grown-ups
—adolescents who listen
—parents who listen
—teachers who teach
—schools that encourage education
—nurses who care
—hospitals who let nurses care
—homes for street people
—peace for terrorists
Welcome to my world.